"The God who sent the Savior to rescue us as individual sinners also cares deeply about the larger world in which we individuals live. And that includes the world of culture—our art, our games, our family patterns, our political systems, and much more. In this excellent and highly readable book, Bruce Ashford spells that out clearly and with much wisdom."

Richard Mouw
Professor of faith and public life, Fuller Theological Seminary

"Bruce Ashford is one of North America's most brilliant theologians. In this book, he proves himself to be a true son of Abraham and Abraham Kuyper. This book will help equip you to think through the questions facing your church and community in the 21st century, including those questions you may not have thought yet to ask."

Russell D. Moore
President, Ethics & Religious Liberty Commission of the
Southern Baptist Convention

"Reading *Every Square Inch* is like reliving my personal journey of discovery, which in many respects, mirrors Bruce Ashford's immersion into another cultural context, viewing the USA from the outside-in, and wondering what Christianity offers regarding the big questions of life, society, and culture. *Every Square Inch* is a splendid introduction to the Christian calling to live under the lordship of Christ in every sphere of life. The gospel is the power of God unto salvation, and its message impacts every area of life. Here is the greatest story ever told (arts) about what the world is truly like (science) now that a crucified messiah is King of the world (politics), a King who has formed a generous people in His image (economics) and now commissions us to teach others to obey all Christ's commands (education)."

Trevin Wax
Managing editor of *The Gospel Project*, author of the
*Gospel-Centered Teaching*, *Clear Winter Nights*, and *Counterfeit Gospels*, and blogger at *Kingdom People*

"In a day in which the Kuyperian tradition is waning in its traditional homelands in North America, it is being recovered and renewed by many evangelicals. Bruce Ashford is one such evangelical. In this fine book Ashford draws on the tradition of Abraham Kuyper and others to articulate an accessible theology of culture for today. Ashford has thought long and hard about these issues and honed creative ways of inducting students into this fertile tradition and he brings all of these strengths into play in this volume. There are few things as critical for our context as the development and practice of a robust, biblical view of cultural engagement. Ashford rightly sets the whole in a missional context and always returns to Scripture as God's infallible Word, while opening the vision on the whole of life as God has made it. This is an important book, and it deserves wide readership!"

Craig G. Bartholomew<br>
H. Evan Runner professor of philosophy and professor of<br>
religion and theology, Redeemer University College

"As in each generation, the Christian has both the privilege and responsibility of spreading everywhere the fragrance of the knowledge of Christ. In a globalized, and increasingly pluralistic context, the task is often easier said than done. Dr. Bruce Ashford exemplifies in his life that grace for the task has been provided, and he excels with his pen in declaring the all-encompassing reign and relevance of the Lord Jesus. As a personal friend and grateful beneficiary of both his life and work on this subject, I commend *Every Square Inch* to all who desire to know how the universal rule of Christ impacts every area of life."

William "Duce" Branch, aka "The Ambassador"<br>
Hip-hop artist, founding member of The Cross Movement

"Bruce Ashford has a real gift to take complicated concepts and put them in words all of us can understand. In *Every Square Inch*, he does just this as he helps us to think Christianly and comprehensively for the glory of Christ in all things. I will be recommending this book for those who want to cultivate a Christian worldview way of thinking and living."

Daniel L. Akin<br>
President, Southeastern Baptist Theological Seminary

# EVERY SQUARE INCH

An Introduction to Cultural
Engagement for Christians

# EVERY SQUARE INCH

An Introduction to Cultural
Engagement for Christians

Bruce Riley Ashford

**LEXHAM PRESS**

**Southeastern**
Baptist Theological Seminary

*Every Square Inch:*
*An Introduction to Cultural Engagement for Christians*

Copyright 2015 Bruce Ashford

Lexham Press, 1313 Commercial St., Bellingham, WA 98225
LexhamPress.com

Print ISBN 978-1-57-799620-0
Digital ISBN 978-1-57-799621-7

Lexham Editorial Team: David Bomar, Lynnea Fraser, Joel Wilcox
Cover Design: Jim LePage
Typesetting: ProjectLuz.com

*For my son, John Paul Kuyper Ashford.*

"Children are a heritage from the LORD."
(Psalm 127:3 ESV)

## TABLE OF CONTENTS

## ACKNOWLEDGMENTS

I wish to thank Brannon Ellis at Lexham Press and Amy Whitfield at Southeastern Baptist Theological Seminary for their commitment to this project. I further wish to thank Greg Forster and his team at the Kern Family Foundation, whose encouragement and support enabled this project to become a reality. I also express gratitude to my friends Devin Maddox and Dennis Greeson, who helped me take ideas that were conceived as a professor at a graduate school and express them in a way that I hope will be helpful for a broader audience.

I am grateful also for friends with whom I've had many discussions about Christianity and culture, including Craig Bartholomew, Dennis Darville, James K. Dew, J. D. Greear, Ken Keathley, Ben Quinn, Heath Thomas, and Keith Whitfield. In addition, I wish to thank Greg Forster, Ken Keathley, Jay W. Richards, and Taylor Worley for providing expert feedback on portions of the manuscript.

Finally, I express love and appreciation for my wife, Lauren, and our three children, Riley Noelle, Anna Katherine, and John Paul Kuyper. Lauren is a constant encouragement in my writing projects—including this one, as she marked off one of our family's two weeks of summer vacation so that I could write the manuscript for this little book. Riley, Anna, and Kuyper are a delight to me and Lauren, and we pray that they will be able to bring the entirety of their lives under submission to Christ's lordship, as a matter of love and worship toward him and as a matter of love and witness toward the world.

I n 1998, at the age of 24, I left the United States for the first time in order to become a university English instructor in Tatarstan, a predominantly Muslim republic in a Central Asian corner of Russia. I had never traveled farther west than San Antonio, farther north than the tip of Maine, farther east than Nags Head (North Carolina), or farther south than Miami. Can you imagine what a never-ending carnival of cultural wedgies the next two years were for me?

My first week in the country, for example, I was introduced to a special drink called "kuhmis," which my buddies told me "will taste a lot like an American milkshake." And truly, it was white and frothy just like a vanilla milkshake. But it turns out that it was white and frothy because it was *fermented mare's milk*. At some point in history, an entrepreneur had decided to milk a horse, allow the milk to rot, and then bottle it as a delicacy. Later that week, I also was served *fish gelatin* for breakfast.

But before long—culinary oddities aside—I was immersed in a cultural context that was a mixture of Eastern European and Central Asian, and which had been shaped in various ways in the past by Sunni Islam and Soviet communism, and more recently by global capitalism and postmodernism. These religious and ideological influences shaped everything in the culture, including the arts, sciences, politics, economic, education, entertainment, family life, and even sports competitions. I found myself wondering what it would look like for me to live a faithfully Christian life in that particular context.

This small book that you are reading is written as a little introduction for Christians who wish to live faithfully in their cultural contexts. It shows how all of life matters to God, and how every Christian can serve powerfully as a representative of Christ, even if he or she is not an international missionary or a pastor. It is meant to show that God cares not only about the goings-on within the four walls of a church building but also about the goings-on in every corner of society and culture. He wants us to take seriously our interactions in the arts (music, literature, cinema, architecture, interior décor, culinary arts), the natural sciences (biology, physics, chemistry), the social sciences (psychology, sociology), the public square (journalism, politics, economics, law), the academy (schools, universities, seminaries), sports and competition, and homemaking. Every dimension of our lives relates in some way to Christ and can in some manner be directed toward him.

## Theology and Culture

In the space of two years in Russia, I began to realize even more fully the deep and resonant effects of religion upon culture, and vice versa. I was living in a social and cultural context that had been almost entirely devoid of evangelical gospel influence for generations. Conversations with many of my students revealed a deep skepticism about whether God existed, whether life had any meaning, and whether there are any moral absolutes. The institutions of this country—including its government, businesses, marriages, and schools—reflected this deep sense of loss, this sense that its people could no longer believe in a God who endowed their lives with meaning and purpose or who gave a moral law by which all people and institutions should abide.

During this time, I began to read books by Christian thinkers such as Abraham Kuyper, Francis Schaeffer, and C. S. Lewis. (On my journey to Russia, I carried one suitcase of clothes and four suitcases of books.) Kuyper lived in 19th-century Holland and served as prime minister of the Netherlands, founded a Christian university, started a newspaper, and wrote influential books on theology, art, science, and many other topics. His deepest convictions might be summed up in one sentence: *Jesus Christ is Lord of all, and because of that fact, every aspect our lives should be affected by the fact that we are Christians.* If Christ is Lord, he is Lord over our work *and* our leisure, our families *and* friendships, our goings-on inside the four walls of a church building *and* outside those walls. He is not just the Lord over certain "religious" things, but Lord over art, science, politics, economics, education, and homemaking. Kuyper gave me my first insight into the fact that Jesus Christ is relevant to every dimension of society and culture, and that for this reason we should allow our Christianity to shape absolutely everything we do.

Francis Schaeffer was an American who lived in Switzerland during the middle of the 20th century. He and his wife, Edith, were known for starting a retreat center—L'Abri—which ministered especially to skeptics and freethinkers, and to those who were hurting spiritually. Schaeffer was known for teaching that the Christian worldview—and it alone—could undergird the full range of human life. What a person believed about Jesus Christ affected that person spiritually, morally, rationally, aesthetically, and relationally. What a society believed about Jesus Christ affected that society in all of its doings—economic, political, ecological, and so forth. Francis and Edith's ministry to seekers and skeptics took place in their own home (L'Abri was founded in their cottage) over dinnertime conversations, evening Q&A sessions, and walks in the Swiss Alps. From the Schaeffers' ministry, I learned not only that Christ is Lord but that he is love. Their way of showing his lordship over all things involved showing his love to all people.

C. S. Lewis was a British professor and writer who taught at Oxford and Cambridge during the middle part of the 20th century. In the scholarly world, he was known for his expertise in medieval literature. In the more popular realm, he was known as the professor who gave radio talks about Christianity during World War II and who wrote popular science fiction, children's fiction, and Christian apologetics. In the years after his death in 1963, he would gain the stature of being one of the most influential Christians of the modern world. His writings remain on the bestseller lists and continue in their own way to shape the world in which we live. From Lewis' life, I learned the powerful effect of Christians shaping their vocations in light of Christ's lordship. Lewis was not a pastor or a missionary. He had a "secular" vocation as a literature professor, and it was precisely in that vocation that he was able to speak about Christ and allow his Christian belief to shape his life and work.

## Spiritual Awakening

As I read books written by and about these three men, I began to find the answers to questions I had been asking for most of my life. Does my Christian belief "hold water" in the real world? Does it make sense out there in the real world of art and science, of politics and economics? Does my Christianity have any impact on my life other than church attendance, personal devotions, and sexual ethics? How does my Christianity matter to my work and my leisure, to my community and political involvement? From Kuyper, Schaeffer, and Lewis, I began to learn just how it is that Christ is Lord over everything, how Christianity matters for every aspect of life. I began to see how Christianity is relevant to every dimension of culture (arts, sciences, public square, the academy, etc.) and to all of our human vocations (not only family and church, but also workplace and community). As Christians, God wants us to live every aspect of our lives in a way that is shaped by our belief that Christ is Lord.

Aside from my conversion, that was probably the most profound spiritual awakening I have ever had, even to this day. In the years since then, I have slowly but steadily built upon the conviction that the Christian mission includes the outworking of the gospel in every dimension of a given culture, in every human vocation, and across the fabric of human existence. Though I've read it or heard it quoted hundreds of times, I am still struck by Kuyper's claim: "Oh, no single piece of our mental world is to be hermetically sealed off from the rest, and there is not a square inch in the whole domain of our human existence over which Christ, who is Sovereign over all, does not cry: 'Mine!' "[1] In *Pro Rege*, Kuyper writes, "The Son [of God] is not to be excluded from anything. You cannot point to any natural realm or star or comet or even descend into the depth of the earth, but it is related to Christ, not in some unimportant tangential way, but directly."[2] God calls us to obey him and witness to him with the totality of our lives.

## The Aim of This Book

I write as an American, to other Americans, in our increasingly post-Christian democratic republic. I aim to equip Christians to think holistically about how the gospel informs everything we do in the world. It is my sincere hope that the barrier we have erected in our hearts between "sacred" and "secular" will be removed, so that we will awaken—perhaps for the first time—to the reality that Jesus is Lord over all of creation—not only the things we consider sacred, but also the things we consider secular.

To that end, *first*, we will examine theological frameworks for understanding culture; *second*, we will establish a biblical, theological account of culture; *third*, we will develop a theology of vocation; *fourth*, we will survey several relevant Christian leaders from history who have made significant contributions to a proper understanding of Christianity and culture; *finally*, we will discuss various spheres of culture from a Christian perspective.

You'll notice that, in the first part of the book, we lay a foundation for the type of Christianity that seeks to be both *in* and *for* culture. We do so, first of all, by distinguishing our view from other views, which understand Christianity as being primarily *against* culture or primarily an agent *of* culture. Next, we show the way in which the Bible's overarching storyline leads us to hold this sort of view. After this, we discuss some Christians throughout church history whose lives, writings, and cultural products provide us with lessons about how to be *in* and *for* our given cultural contexts. Finally, we discuss the various God-given callings that serve as the major media through which we engage our culture. To summarize the message of the first part of the book, we want to live our lives firmly in the midst of our cultural contexts, living in such a way that we shape our words and actions in light of the Christian gospel and direct others to look at the Lord whom we admire. We want to speak of him with our lips and reflect him with our lives so that tapestry of the Christian community's (cultural) life is seamlessly and beautifully woven with compellingly Christian words and deeds.

One of the questions that immediately arises, however, is how to do that in the diverse arenas of culture in which we find ourselves. How do we apply our view of cultural engagement when we find ourselves in particular situations? Where do we even begin to think through what it means to please God in the realms of art, science, or politics? What does it mean to be a "Christian" teacher, scholar, or economist? The chapters in the last half of this book are designed to give brief but enlightening starting points for Christians who want to begin answering these sorts of questions.

Because these questions are so profound and the answers to them so interesting and so expansive, each of the topics in the last half of the book could easily demand that an entire book be written just to introduce each of them. For that reason, I will not be able to provide a comprehensive introduction to each topic. Instead, I will pick an aspect of each topic that I think will be interesting to a broad audience, and then I will provide a very brief and hopefully helpful discussion about that aspect of the topic.

To aid in our discussion, I have added recommended reading and discussion questions at the end of each chapter. Though this book is suitable for individual use, it is also appropriately read in community with others. Because the Christian life is social in nature, the discussion questions about culture in this book are best discussed with others who are reading it. Furthermore, I hope this isn't the final book you read on theology and culture. Each chapter is filled with relevant material to guide you to read more deeply on a variety of topics.

To close, I am reminded of a quote by Father John Richard Neuhaus, founder of *First Things* magazine. Neuhaus said,

"Barrels of ink have been spilt in trying to define what is meant by culture, and I do not presume to have the final word on the subject."[3]

Like Neuhaus, I do not claim to have cornered the market on "culture." But I do aim to serve you well as you developing your own theological framework for seeing all of life under the lordship of Christ.

# CHAPTER 1

# Competing Views on Theology and Culture

My second week in the former Soviet Union, I was introduced to the *banya*. My buddies told me that it "will be a lot like an American sauna." And sure enough, it was a square room with a lot of heat. But there were a few differences. One difference lay in the fact that steam was generated by pouring *vodka* onto a barrel full of hot coals. (I wanted to join in, but as a Baptist I didn't have any vodka and couldn't find my bottle of Nyquil.) Another difference lay in the fact that many of these "saunas" have bundles of birch branches in the corner, with which the men *whip one another on the back,* starting at the heels and working methodically and consistently up to the shoulders. Afterward, they go outside the *banya* and roll around in the snow. I'm not kidding. I've never prayed so hard for the Second Coming.

Aside from a few odd moments, such as the one I just described, I thoroughly enjoyed the experience of being immersed in a very complex culture, one that was a multilayered synthesis of Soviet-era atheism, Central Asian Islam, global capitalism, and postmodernism. On Friday evenings, I could pay a dollar to attend world-class symphonies and piano concerts at the performing arts center one mile from my apartment. On weekday mornings, I took language lessons in Russian and Tatar, discovering how human languages provide unique categories for thinking and unique advantages and disadvantages for mediating the gospel. On weekday afternoons, I taught at three universities that were cultural legacies of years past. In the evenings, I drank hot tea (the manly drink of choice in Central Asia, best imbibed with a spot of milk and a spoon of sugar) and watched snow fall on a mosque and an Eastern Orthodox cathedral that stood just outside my apartment window. Often, I had a huddle of undergrad or grad students in my apartment, asking me questions about why I believe in God (atheists) or how in the world I could believe that a man was God (Muslims).

As an evangelical, Protestant American living in a part of Russia populated mostly by Central Asian Muslims, I was forced to live in a cultural context that was different in many ways from the one in which I had grown up. There were some aspects of this culture that I preferred to my home context, and some that I did not. There were things that I embraced easily, and things that I did not. The question that kept surfacing, however, was: "How should I, as an evangelical Christian, approach 'culture'?" In other words, is culture something good or bad? On the one hand, is it something I should try to escape or avoid, or against which

I should fight? On the other hand, is it something I should embrace? Or is there some third and better alternative?

When it comes to interacting with culture, Christians face a choice between several options. One option is to live a life that can be characterized as "Christianity *against* culture," which views culture as something that a person tries to escape from or fight against. Another option could be called "Christianity *of* culture," which views culture uncritically as something that can be accepted wholesale into a person's life and church. A final option can be called "Christianity *in and for* culture," in which a believer seeks to live Christianly *within* his or her cultural context and for the betterment of that context, while not rejecting it wholesale, on the one hand, or accepting it wholesale, on the other. The remainder of this chapter, and in fact the whole book, will attempt to articulate what it might look like for American Christians to live out their faith in the midst of their particular cultural contexts.

## What Is Culture?

Before going any further, however, we should take a moment to discuss what we mean when we talk about "culture." When some people talk about culture, what they really mean is "high culture," because they have in mind sophisticated cultural products such as Beethoven's music or Rembrandt's paintings. When other people talk about culture, what they really mean is "popular culture," because they have in mind everyday cultural products such as television shows, movies, or Top 40 songs. Still others use the word "culture" to refer to anything that is *against* what they believe as a Christian.

Unlike these three senses of the word "culture," the meaning I have in mind is all-encompassing. "Culture" is anything that humans produce when they interact with each other and with God's creation. When we interact with each other and with God's creation, we cultivate the ground (grain, vegetables, livestock), produce artifacts (clothes, housing, cars), build institutions (governments, businesses, schools), form worldviews (theism, pantheism, atheism), and participate in religions (Christianity, Hinduism, Buddhism, Islam, Atheism). We produce culture, and at the same time our cultural context shapes us, affecting who we are, what we think and do, and how we feel.

So the concept of culture is very broad, encompassing in one way or another the totality of our life in this world. For this reason, we don't want to "get it wrong" in figuring out a Christian's relationship to culture. If we get the relationship right, it will positively transform our lives and the world around us, but if we get it wrong, it will deform our lives and the world around us.

Now that we have a basic grasp of what culture is, we are prepared to outline three models for relating Christianity and culture. As I am describing these models, you will probably be able to place yourself and other Christians you know in one of the categories.

## Christianity *against* Culture

**Some proponents of "Christianity *against* culture" tend to view the Church primarily as a bomb shelter.** This is especially a temptation for Americans who realize that their country is becoming increasingly post-Christian—and, in some ways, even anti-Christian. They realize that their beliefs on certain theological and moral issues will increasingly be rejected and mocked by the political and cultural elite and by many of their fellow citizens.

Under such an ideological assault, Christians sometimes have a collective anxiety attack. Their dominant mood tends to be protective, conceiving the Church as a bomb shelter trying to protect believers from aerial assault, or perhaps a monastery where people can withdraw from the contingencies of contemporary existence—or even better, a perpetual yoga retreat where we can empty our minds of certain harsh realities.

Believers with this mentality have good intentions. They want to preserve the church's purity, recognizing that the church is under attack and that therefore we should hold fast to the faith (Rev 3:11). They know that there is a great battle being waged (Eph 6), a battle that plays out both invisibly in the heavenly realm, and visibly in the cultural realm.

However, this mentality is misguided, arising from a timid fear of humanity; it is spurred more by secular wisdom than by biblical faith, more by faithless fear than by Christian courage and vitality. It views the church as a walled city rather than a living being, as a safe-deposit box rather than a conduit of spiritual power. It externalizes godlessness and treats it as something that can be kept out by man-made walls, rather than understanding that godlessness is a disease of the soul that can never be walled out. This mindset tends toward legalism and tries to restrict Christians' interactions with society and culture. While it rightly recognizes that the Christian life involves war against the powers of darkness, it wrongly tries to wage that war by escaping from the world. This obeys only one half of Jesus' admonition to be in the world, but not of it (John 17:14–16).

**Other proponents of "Christianity *against* culture" view the Church primarily as an Ultimate Fighter.** The Ultimate-Fighter mentality shares much in common with the bomb-shelter mentality, but it deals with its anxiety in a different manner. It tends to see Christians exclusively and comprehensively as fighters, whose weapons are beliefs, feelings, and values wielded in spiritual warfare. Unlike those hiding in the bomb shelter, the fighters venture forth into the surrounding culture, seeking greater awareness of it so that they might assault it with lethal force.

Believers with this mentality are clinging to the biblical principle of waging war against what is evil. They rightly recognize that we must put on the whole armor of God (Eph 6:11), fight the good fight of faith (1 Tim 6:12), resist the devil (Jas 4:7), and cast down anything that exalts itself against God (2 Cor 10:4–5).

However, this mentality is misguided to the extent that it wrongly applies the principles above. The fault of the Ultimate-Fighter Church (UFC) is not that it wants to fight, but that it suggests that the entirety of the Christian life is nothing but war. Our social and cultural contexts are full of unbelievers—but those unbelievers are not only enemies of God, but also drowning people in need of a lifeboat. The church is not only a base for soldiers, but also a hospital for the sick. The Christian life is surely a battle, but it is no less a journey, a joy, an adventure, and a trust. In other words, Christians must indeed fight, but that is not the only thing they do; their battling is done from within the broader context of the entire Christian life.

## Christianity *of* Culture

**Those with a "Christianity *of* culture" perspective tend to build churches that are mirrors of the culture.** Christians with this mindset tend to view their cultural context in very high esteem—perhaps disagreeing with aspects of it here and there, but for the most part finding it to be an ally rather than a threat. They tend to interact easily and uncritically with the dominant philosophical, political, and cultural trends of the day. Unlike those who seek to escape from culture or to fight it with lethal force, they seek to incorporate the dominant culture seamlessly into their lives and churches.

Believers with this mentality rightly recognize that God ordered the world in such a way that humans would make culture, and they rightly recognize that their culture exhibits real aspects of truth, goodness, and beauty. However, this mentality is misguided because it fails to sufficiently see the way in which every culture, and every aspect of culture, is corrupted and distorted because of human sin. When Christians adopt a "Christianity *of* culture" mindset, they take away Christianity's ability to be a prophetic voice and usually end up sacrificing doctrines and moral beliefs that run contrary to the cultural consensus. This mindset comes at too high of a cost, as it ends up subverting the historical Christian faith.

## Christianity *in* and *for* Culture

**We live *in* and *for* our cultural context.** A third and better mindset is one that views human beings as representatives of Christ who live their lives *in* the midst of and *for* the good of their cultural context, and whose cultural lives are characterized by obedience and witness.

Every culture possesses some inherent goodness. God ordered the world in such a way that people spontaneously make culture, and the very existence of music, art, food, housing, and education represent a fundamental human good. Furthermore, God has enabled all people—Christian or not—to make good and valuable contributions in the cultural realm. But under this view, the Christian also recognizes that every culture is corrupted and misdirected. Since the time of the first couples' sin, all human beings sin, and our sin corrupts our cultural efforts. We are idolaters—people who worship things that ought not to be worshipped, such as sex, money, and power—and the cultural realities we produce tend to be directed toward those idols rather than toward Christ. So God structured the world so that it would be a cultural world, but we humans have misdirected our cultural realities. Every cultural context is *structurally* good, but *directionally* corrupt. For this reason, we must live firmly in the midst of our cultural contexts (structurally), all the while seeking to steer our cultural realities toward Christ rather than toward idols (directionally).

In order to help us think clearly about the cultural aspect of our mission, let me explain more precisely what I mean by "structure" and "direction." When God created the world, it was a "good" world both structurally and directionally. The way God designed the world (its structures) was good, and the way humanity used his world was good (it honored God and was directed toward him).

After the fall, the world remained structurally good but became directionally bad. The world is still good in its design (structure), but human beings use the world in ways that are oriented toward self-worship and the worship of things rather than God (direction). We live in a fallen world. Our tendency as humans is to worship things like sex, money, and power, rather than worshiping God. And when we worship idols like this, it affects our social and cultural activities. Our activities are misdirected, being aimed toward idols rather than toward God. As Christians, we want to speak out against this misdirection of God's world. But in speaking out *against* the world, we are doing the best possible thing *for* the world. We are being against the world for the sake of the world.

Because of Christ's redemption, we are new creatures. God has transformed us so that we live in an entirely different manner than we did before. That transformation affects all of the things we do, including our cultural activities. For this reason, our mission as Christians includes identifying the ways in which our cultures are corrupted and misdirected by sin, and then doing everything in our power to help bring healing and redirection to them. When we do this, we are obeying Christ and being a witness.

**We do this as a matter of obedience.** If Christ is the creator of everything, then we must realize that his lordship is as wide as creation. Nothing in this universe escapes his lordship. And if his lordship is as wide as creation, then our obedience to his lordship must be as wide as culture. The call to be disciples of Christ is the call to bring absolutely every square inch of the fabric of our lives under his lordship.

**We do this also as a matter of witness.** Every aspect of human life and culture is ripe for Christian witness. Every dimension of culture, whether it is art, science, or politics, is an arena in which we can speak about Christ with our lips and reflect him with our lives. We thank God for the existence of culture and recognize whatever is good in it, while at the same time seeking to redirect whatever is not good toward Christ.

We realize that we will never "win" by transforming our culture in such a way that it glorifies Christ comprehensively or enduringly. God never promises victory until Christ returns and secures the victory for himself. But he does command us to obey him and bear witness to him by doing everything within our powers to direct our cultural activities toward Christ.

## A Preview of the Kingdom

When Christ returns, he will return as the victorious King. Until that time, the Christian community should live its life as a seamless tapestry of *word* and *deed*. When we witness and obey in this manner, we benefit the world by serving as a preview of God's coming kingdom. We proclaim Christ and the gospel with our lips (word), and we promote Christ and the gospel with our lives (deed). In so doing, we offer to the world a preview of that future era when Christ rules the new heavens and earth—the era in which all social and cultural realities will be directed toward Christ. In that era, we will have right relationship with God, each other, and the created order, and our social and cultural activities will be perfect and resplendent reflections of Christ.

Absolutely everything in life matters to God. He cares not only about the goings-on within the four walls of a congregational gathering, but also about the goings-on in other corners of society and culture. We must live Christianly not only as the Church *gathered* on Sunday morning for worship, but also as the Church *scattered* into the world in our work, leisure, and community life. We must take seriously our interactions in the arts, the sciences, the public square, and the academy.

When we as the Church live our lives in such a way that everything we do and say points to God, our combined witness serves as an attractive preview of God's coming kingdom. In that kingdom, there will be no more pain or tears, no more sin or the consequences of sin. In that kingdom, we will be in right relationship with God, with each other, and with all of creation. There is no greater calling in life than to live as a preview of that kingdom.

While I was living abroad in Russia, it would have been easy to fall in love with my new culture (Christianity *of* culture). Admittedly, part of the draw of living overseas is the opportunity to experience new cultural realities. But it would have been equally tempting, particularly during seasons of loneliness and isolation or when encountering some aspect of the culture that was hostile to my Christian faith, to despise the culture as a whole (Christianity *against* culture). My goal—and I hope you share the same goal—was neither to idolize nor to despise the culture I was on a mission to serve. My goal was to reflect the transformative power of God *in* and *for* the culture, to the glory of God.

## Action Points

- Many of us live "compartmentalized lives," having areas that we feel Jesus cares about, and other areas that we feel he ignores. What are some areas of your life that you have never considered as pertaining to Jesus and his lordship. Why?

- As I mentioned earlier, the Christian life is often a battle, and yet it is also to be characterized by care for the "sick and wounded." What are some things you see in your cultural context that Christians are called to fight against? Are there times when it is better not to fight? How do you tell the difference?

- As Christians living in a fallen world, we often face the temptation to be Christians "against culture" who view the church as a bomb shelter or an Ultimate Fighter, or to be Christians "of culture" who capitulate by conforming ourselves to the culture. Can you think of contemporary examples of these two flawed approaches?

## Recommended Reading

Crouch, Andy. *Culture Making: Recovering our Creative Calling.* Downers Grove, IL: InterVarsity Press, 2008. An engaging and persuasive treatise on the Christian community's calling to "make culture" rather than merely "engage the culture."

Forster, Greg. *Joy for the World: How Christianity Lost Its Cultural Influence and Can Begin Rebuilding It.* Wheaton, IL: Crossway, 2014. A well-written and easy-to-read book arguing that the key to cultural transformation is Spirit-induced joy in God and the gospel.

Hunter, James Davison. *To Change the World: Irony, Tragedy, and Possibility of Christianity in the Late Modern World.* Oxford: Oxford University Press, 2010. A sociologist argues that Christians should aim to be a "faithful presence" in their culture.

Kuyper, Abraham. *Lectures on Calvinism.* 1898. Reprint, Grand Rapids: Eerdmans, 1943. In this small book, Kuyper argues that our Christianity should affect every sphere of human life and culture.

Mouw, Richard J. *Called to Holy Worldliness*. Philadelphia: Fortress, 1980. A small book showing how ordinary Christians can honor God in their culture-making and cultural engagement.

Niebuhr, H. Richard. *Christ and Culture*. New York: HarperCollins, 1956. This text has become the modern benchmark for discussing Christianity and culture. It has flaws—serious ones—but is worth reading.

Smith, James K. A. *Desiring the Kingdom*. Grand Rapids: Baker Academic, 2009. A more advanced book which argues that secular "liturgies" compete with Christian liturgies in order to shape who we are and form our deepest identities and views of the world.

# A Theology of Culture

In the previous chapter, we encountered three different approaches to Christianity and culture and concluded that Christians should be "in and for" the culture rather than primarily "of" it or "against" it. We argued that Christians should try to discern the way in which any cultural reality is corrupted and misdirected by sin and idolatry, and then seek to redirect that reality toward Christ. We do this as a matter of obedience and witness, proclaiming Christ with our lips and promoting him with our lives, in the hope that we can serve as a preview of his coming kingdom.

But where in the Bible is this view of Christianity and culture promoted? In this chapter, I will articulate a basic theology of culture under the categories of creation, fall, redemption, and new creation. These four categories are the four "plot movements" of the Bible's big story, and any view of culture must vindicate itself in relation to these categories.

## Why a Theology of Culture Is Necessary

Evangelical Christians often talk about engaging the culture, contextualizing the gospel, and speaking prophetically to our culture. However, from my experience, not many of us have taken the time to build a biblical theology of culture. Although we usually operate (consciously or unconsciously) with some sort of idea of what culture is and what the Bible says about it, often we haven't drawn upon the major biblical building blocks in order to construct a thoroughly evangelical theology of culture.

When we fail to consciously, actively develop a theology of culture, we operate on whatever theology is closest in proximity. Perhaps it is the theology of culture we have picked up tacitly from popular films. Maybe it comes from a family member. Or perhaps, if one is fortunate, it comes from childhood sermons. Regardless, and without knowing, we make decisions in every sphere of life that are informed by theology that has not been vetted by Scripture and our consciences. It is vital, therefore, that we examine our doctrine for the purpose of faithful living. For this reason, we will now turn to the Scriptures for a basic overview of our topic.

## Creation

The Bible's opening narrative tells us about God's creation, including God's design for human culture. In the very first chapters, we are told that God created the heavens and the earth. He created out of nothing, he shaped what he created, and he called the work of his hands "good." At each step along the way, the narrative affirms the goodness of God's handiwork. Moreover, when God completes his creation by making humanity in his image and likeness, the narrative affirms that God's creation was "very good" (Gen 1:31).

Humans are the culmination of God's good creation. They are different from God's other handiwork. Indeed, the first statement about humans is that God made them in the image and likeness of God, male and female alike. They are like God in many ways, including but not limited to their capacities for spirituality, morality, relationality, language, rationality, and creativity. Man's likeness to God, John Calvin argues, "extends to the whole excellence by which man's nature towers over all the kinds of living creatures."[1] Because of these capacities, God could place the man and woman in the garden to have dominion over God's good creation (Gen 1:26–27) and to work it and keep it (Gen 2:15).

Pause for a moment to reflect on the fact that God's command to work was a command to change and even enhance what he had made. Adam and Eve were not supposed to leave God's creation as it was, but to make something out of it. They and their descendants would be able to "work the garden" not only by cultivating plant life (agri-culture), but also by cultivating the arts, the sciences, or the public square (culture in general).

What, then, does the creation narrative contribute to a discussion of culture? First, human culture is part of the physical and material world, which is part of God's creation before the fall and therefore is not inherently bad. We must not allow ourselves to fall into a form of neo-gnosticism, treating "spiritual" things as good and "material" things as bad. We may not take a dualist[2] view of the creation, with its attendant impulse toward comprehensive cultural separation and withdrawal; to do so is to adopt a hollow and deceptive philosophy, to denigrate God's good creation and, implicitly, to undermine the incarnation.

Second, God gave humans the capacities to create culture and then commanded them to use those capacities. God created humans in his image and likeness, thereby giving them capacities for spirituality, morality, relationality, language, rationality, and creativity. Then he *commanded* them to use those gifts (e.g., Gen 2:15; Exod 31:1–11).

## Fall

God's creation of the world is the opening scene of the Scriptures and constitutes the first major plot movement of the overarching biblical narrative. Immediately after this opening scene, however, Adam and Eve rebelled against God, seeking to set themselves up as autonomous. The effect of this sin for them, and for all of humanity, was disastrous (Rom 1:18–32). People no longer live in paradise, but instead live in a world pervaded by sin and its effects. Man's relationship with God was broken, as well as his relationship with himself, with others, and with the rest of the created order.

In Romans 1, Paul describes the result of humanity's broken relationship with *God*, pointing out that people now worship the creature rather than the Creator (Rom 1:25).

The image of God in humanity is now distorted and defaced. However, people are alienated not only from God, but also from *others* (Rom 1:28–31). Rather than loving their neighbors as themselves, they lie, murder, rape, and otherwise demean their fellow imagers (e.g., Gen 9:6). Furthermore, they are alienated from the *created order*, as their attempts to "work the garden" are full of frustration and pain (Gen 3:17–18). Finally, they are alienated even from *themselves*, as life becomes meaningless because of their separation from God (Eccl 1:1–11).

The implications of the fall for a discussion of human culture are massive. Sin defiles everything. Spiritually, humans are idolaters, worshiping God's gifts instead of worshiping God himself (Col 3:5). Rationally, they have difficulty discerning the truth, and they use their capacities to construct vain philosophies (Rom 1:18–21). Creatively, they use their imagination to create and worship idols rather than to worship the living God (Isa 40:18–20). Relationally, they use their power to exploit others and serve themselves (Gen 5:8). As a result, any and all human culture is distorted and defaced by sin. No dimension of culture is left unscathed by sin's pervasive reach.

The fall and its consequences do not, however, make God's creation (or, by implication human culture) inherently bad. Even though the world is corrupted by sin, it is still materially good. Recognizing this frees us from false asceticisms and gnosticisms that view the use and enjoyment of God's creation as wrong. As Al Wolters puts it, God's creation remains *structurally* good, although since the fall it is *directionally* corrupt.[3] Structure refers to the order of creation, while direction refers to the order of sin and redemption. The directional results of the fall, for human culture, are revealed in such things as poor reasoning in the realm of science, *kitsch* in the realm of art, and hatred in the realm of relationships.

Anything in creation can be directed toward God or away from him. It is this directionality that distinguishes between the good and the bad, between worship and idolatry, rather than some distinction between spiritual and material. We should note, however, that in spite of the fall, things are not as bad as they could be. Without common grace and the Spirit's restraining work, this world would be an utter horror, and because of God's grace through his Spirit after the fall, we may continue to produce culture, thereby using our uniquely human capacities.

## Redemption and New Creation

The Bible's third plot movement occurs immediately after the fall. God gives not only a promise of death (Gen 2:17), but also a promise of life (Gen 3:15). He immediately declares that one day the offspring of the woman would destroy the serpent. Paul recognizes this promise as a prophecy of Jesus Christ (Gal 3:16), God's Son who is "born of a woman" (Gal 4:4). This declaration, therefore, is God's promise to send the Messiah. Ultimately, the entirety of Scripture testifies about this Messiah, as its pages declare how God, in spite of seemingly insurmountable obstacles, would fulfill his promise to send this Savior.

God affirms that by the Savior's wounds man is healed, and upon the Savior's shoulders the sin of the world was borne (Isa 52:13–53:12). Furthermore, the redemption he provides reaches into every square inch of God's creation, including the non-human aspects of creation. This redemption of the created order is made clear in major christological and soteriological passages such as Colossians 1:13–23 and Ephesians 1:3–14. In the Colossians text, we are told that Christ the creator of all things is also Christ the reconciler of all things; God will work "by [Christ] to reconcile all things to Himself, by Him" (Col 1:20 NKJV). In the Ephesians passage, we are told that we have redemption through Christ's blood, and that, furthermore, "in the dispensation of the fullness of the times He might gather together in one all things in Christ, both which are in heaven and which are on earth—in Him" (Eph 1:10 NKJV). We know that Christ has not yet reconciled all things to himself because creation still groans in bondage (Rom 8:20–22).

For this reason, Scripture points us forward to a new heavens and earth in which God's kingdom will be realized. At the beginning of the Scriptures, we learn that God created the heavens and the earth (Gen 1:1), while at the end we see him giving us a "new heavens and a new earth" (Isa 65:17; Rev 21:1). At the beginning, we are told of a garden, but in the end we are told of a beautiful city that is cultural through and through, replete with precious metals and jewels and the treasures of the nations (Rev 21). Christ's redemptive work extends beyond God's *people* to God's *cosmos*, so that in the end "creation itself will be set free from its bondage to decay and obtain the freedom of the glory of the children of God" (Rom 8:21). This world will be one "in which righteousness dwells" (2 Pet 3:13 NKJV), thus fulfilling God's good purposes for his world.

Therefore, the final two plot movements tell the story of God redeeming both his imagers and his creation. Two cultural implications are important to notice. First, the doctrines of redemption and restoration are confluent with the doctrine of creation in affirming the goodness of God's creation. God values his creation, and in the end times he will not reject it. Instead, he will restore it, renewing the heavens and earth so that they give him glory. Furthermore, he promises to give us glorified bodies in that day (1 Cor 15:20–28, 50–58). While God could have promised man an eternity floating around in a bodiless state, in some sort of ethereal wonderland, instead he promises to give man a resurrected bodily existence in a restored universe that shines with the glory of God himself (Rev 21:1–4, 9–11). This promise is yet more reason to view God's creation as good, and our faithful cultural interaction with it as something that pleases God.

Second, the doctrine of restoration is confluent with the doctrine of creation in its affirmation of the value of faithful culture-work. Because God (in the beginning) values his good creation and commands humanity to produce culture, and because he promises (in the end) to give us a glorious creation replete with its own culture, we ought to live culturally in a manner consistent with God's designs. "The difference between the Christian hope of resurrection and a mythological hope," writes Dietrich Bonhoeffer, "is that the Christian hope sends a man back to his life on earth in a wholly new way."[4] This new way includes glorifying God from within our cultural contexts, providing a sign of the already-and-not-yet kingdom—of what the world will be like one day when all of creation and culture praises him. As we interact within various dimensions of culture—the arts, the sciences, education, public square, etc.—we are called to do so by bringing the gospel to bear upon those dimensions.

In our evangelism and church-planting, we must recognize that the gospel is always proclaimed, the church is always planted, and the Christian life is always lived within a cultural context (through human language, oratory, music, categories of thought, etc.). Instead of chafing against this reality, we may delight in our charge to make the gospel at home in those cultures, and to allow the gospel to critique them and bring them under the scrutiny of God's revelation. In the words of D. A. Carson:

> We await the return of Jesus Christ, the arrival of the new heaven and the new earth, the dawning of the resurrection, the glory of perfection, the beauty of holiness. Until that day, we are a people in tension. On the one hand, we belong to the broader culture in which we find ourselves; on the other, we belong to the culture of the consummated kingdom of God, which has dawned upon us."

God restores his creation instead of trashing it and expects us to minister within our cultural context rather than attempting to extract ourselves from it.

## Action Points

- Christians are said to live "between two worlds," recognizing God's work in the present fallen world and anticipating the full completion of his work in the new heavens and new earth. What are some specific examples of how our lives in this present era can give the world a glimpse of the future era, the new heavens and earth?

- The end view of God's redemption is the created order as it was always meant to be. In a way, humans will finally be all that it means to be human. God's redemption has the whole creation in view, including the whole person. How does this affect the Christian life? How should this guide our evangelism and caring for people through the different ministries of the church?

- God declares his creation good. In and of itself, therefore, creation is not evil. However, sin misdirects God's good creation. What types of things does this realization lead us to affirm? List three elements of culture and consider how they can be directed toward God or away from him.

- If all humanity is created in the image of God, and if that image is not lost in the fall, then what does that means for how we view and treat other people?

## Recommended Reading

Goheen, Mike and Craig Bartholomew. *Living at the Crossroads: An Introduction to Christian Worldview.* Grand Rapids: Baker Academic, 2008. This book is a fine treatment of how the biblical narrative fosters a worldview that in turn shapes the entirety of the Christian life, including especially culture-making and cultural engagement.

Wittmer, Michael E. *Heaven Is a Place on Earth: Why Everything You Do Matters to God.* Grand Rapids: Zondervan, 2004. A very accessible treatment of the Bible's teaching about culture.

# CHAPTER 3

# Culture and Calling

H as anyone ever asked you, "What do you want to be when you grow up?" In a nation of adults who are all former career-day audience members, it's easy to see why Americans tend to judge their worth based upon their workplace success or the type of career they have.

Or take, for example, the epitome of dinner-party small talk: "So, what do you do?" We introduce who we *are* by what we *do*. More times than not, we equate our identity with our workplace vocation.

Now, that's not to say that what we do is irrelevant to who we are—quite the contrary! In fact, it's not bad to ask children, "What do you want to be when you grow up?" as long as you help them understand that their identity and worth are not bound up exclusively with their 9-to-5 career.

As we noted in the first chapter, "culture" is quite broad as a concept, covering various "spheres" or "dimensions" or "arenas"—such as art, science, business, sports and competition, scholarship and education, homemaking, entertainment, and politics. So the concept of culture encompasses in one way or another the totality of our lives in this world.

Closely related to these arenas of culture are vocations, which serve as the medium through which we interact in those arenas. Vocation comes from the Latin word *vocatio*, which means "calling." One of Christianity's most famous pastors, Martin Luther, is known for applying his biblical sermons to his congregation's vocations. Luther was right to recognize that God gives Christians multiple callings—to churches, families, workplaces, and communities. In this chapter, we will discuss these four callings, which enable us to honor Christ in various arenas of culture.

In an excellent book titled *God at Work*, Gene Veith takes his cues from Luther and explains that the purpose of each of these callings is to love the Lord our God and to love our neighbors as ourselves (Mark 12:30–31).[1] We demonstrate our love for God by fulfilling these callings in ways that honor him, bring him glory, and are shaped by his Word. We demonstrate our love for our neighbors similarly, by exercising our callings in ways that honor God and are shaped by his Word. Our love for God leads to love for our neighbors. In fulfilling our callings, we will notice that we are loving our neighbors and they are loving us. Through our callings, we serve our neighbors and they serve us. We depend upon them, and they depend upon us.

Consider the example of a hungry child. When God provides for a hungry child, he usually does not do so by sending manna from heaven, or by instantaneously multiplying fishes and loaves. Although in certain instances he might do such things, ordinarily he does not. Ordinarily, God feeds hungry children through the work of farmers.

In the United States, the children's food most likely is grown on a farm, shipped to a warehouse, and then delivered to grocery stores, where parents buy food for their children. So far, the hungry child has been fed because of the work of farmers, tractor designers, truck drivers, warehouse owners, grocery store clerks, parents, and many others. But if we look a little deeper, we'll also realize that the grocery store itself was built by engineers, contractors, electricians, and plumbers. The quality of food was (hopefully) overseen by public health inspectors. To summarize, God ordinarily feeds hungry children through a vast network of people who are fulfilling their vocations. The same can be said about the way God ordinarily heals sick people, provides shelter for families, or supplies any number of other necessities and conveniences.

Notice in the example above that these callings are accomplished by human "hands," but they are also the "gloves" into which God slips his divine hand in order to care for his world. A parent provides for a child's physical hunger (a parent's calling to a family) with food that originated at a farm (the farmer's calling to a workplace) and was purchased with the parent's paycheck (the parent's calling to a workplace) from a grocery store located in their town (the parent's calling to a community), and then the parent teaches that child to learn to fulfill her spiritual hunger by becoming a disciple in a community of believers (the child's calling to a church).

## Family

A child's first experience of God's provision usually comes through his or her family. As Gene Veith puts it, in the family we find "the most basic of all vocations, the one in which God's creative power and his providential care are most dramatically conveyed through human beings."[2] The Bible's teaching about marriage and family is rich and profound. Paul compares the relationship between a man and woman to the relationship between Christ and the Church. A husband and wife should consciously strive to make their marriage one that gives their children, and anybody else who might be watching, a picture of Christ's love for the Church, and of Christians' love for Christ. The Proverbs and other writings teach us that parents are responsible for teaching their children how to live wisely under God's lordship. From experience, we see that the way children learn to honor their father and mother also is a step on the path toward learning how to honor their heavenly Father; likewise, children who learn to love their family members are also learning to love other people they will encounter in the world. So the calling to a family is significant, and it shapes a person from childhood until death.

## Church

After God raised his Son from the dead, Jesus appeared to his disciples and promised to empower them through the Holy Spirit, so that they could be his witnesses to the world (Acts 1:8). When the Spirit came upon the disciples, as Jesus had promised, the first thing he did was empower them to win people to Christ and to form churches that ministered to them through teaching and learning, worship, fellowship, and witness (Acts 2:40–47). We learn from the New Testament that God's intention is for believers to be disciples in the midst of these committed communities of believers that we call churches.

The Bible describes the Church by using various images. Peter describes the Church as the *people of God*, reminding us that we are God's possession, and that we are a community rather than merely a collection of individuals (1 Pet 2:9–10). Paul describes the Church as the *body of Christ*. He uses this image to refer sometimes to the Church universal (Eph 1:20–23) and sometimes to the church local (1 Cor 12:27). This image helps us to understand that we are many members but one body (unity and diversity) and that each of us belongs to the other members of the body (mutual love and interdependence). Peter and Paul both describe the Church as the *temple of the Spirit*. Our body is a temple of the Spirit (1 Cor 6:19), and we are living stones built into a spiritual house (1 Pet 2:5). One of the things this image does is remind us that we as believers are held together by the Spirit.

Numerous other Bible passages illuminate for us the way in which our calling to a church teaches us how to be Christian. One example is the "one another" commands. We are told to live in harmony with one another (Rom 12:16; 15:5), forgive and bear with one another (Col 3:13), and not pass judgment on one another (Rom 14:1). We must admonish and encourage one another (1 Thess 5:14), care for one another (1 Cor 12:25), and comfort one another (2 Cor 13:11). Perhaps all of the many "one another" commands could be summed up in 1 Thessalonians 5:15: "Always pursue what is good for one another and for all" (NET). These commands, which are given to all of the members of the church, show that we are all responsible to one another and ultimately to Christ.

So our calling to a church teaches us to love God and to love one another. It reminds us that we are God's possession, that we are a community rather than a mere collection of individuals, and that we are a unity-in-diversity that is held together by the Spirit. It teaches us to love one another even when it is not comfortable to do so, and it shapes us through its ministries of teaching and learning, worship, fellowship, and witness. When the church lives and witnesses together in this manner, it serves as a window into which the world can peer in order to see Christ, and it serves as a "boot camp" that equips and trains its members to go out into the world and witness to Christ both in word and in deed.

## Workplace

Some Christians view their workplaces merely as a way to put bread on the table, as drudgeries that they endure in order to provide a paycheck for their families. But the biblical portrayal of work is much deeper and more profound. In the first place, the Bible portrays God as a worker who made the world in which we live and who in fact made *us*. Because of his work, we exist in this world. But second, the

Bible portrays work as essential to our humanity, as his first words to humanity included admonitions to till the soil, name the animals, and manage the world that God had created.

In fact, the Bible portrays God and man as cooperative workers. God continues to provide for the world (God is a worker) and often does so precisely through our human workplaces (we are workers). This sort of cooperation can be seen in Psalm 90:7, which says that God is the one who establishes the work of our hands. The British pastor John Stott writes, "This concept of divine-human collaboration applies to all honorable work. God has so ordered life on earth as to depend on us. ... So whatever our work, we need to see it as being ... cooperation with God. ... It is this that glorifies him."[3] When we obey God's calling in our workplaces, we are actively cooperating with him as he provides for the world.

This should come as good news, because most of us spend the majority of our waking hours at our workplaces, whether we work as entrepreneurs, teachers, or homemakers. During those hours, we make many relationships, interact in various arenas of culture, and use many of our God-given abilities simply through doing our jobs. It would be a shame to waste our jobs by doing those things in a merely repetitive manner marked by drudgery rather than by happy obedience to God and in purposeful witness to those who are watching.

When we view our workplaces as "callings" from God, we recognize that they are amazing opportunities for witness and obedience. When we obey God by doing our jobs in a way that glorifies him, we find that our jobs are opportunities to speak about Christ and to shape our work toward him. In other words, our jobs are opportunities to witness about Christ precisely by backing up our words with actions. Not only do we let people know verbally that Christ is Lord, but we also do our work in a way that is shaped by Christ and his Word. This combination of word and deed can be powerful. For many people, the workplace is their best opportunity to meet unbelievers who might have never heard the gospel or seen a Christian living out the gospel in front of their very eyes.

## Community

Another calling that we often neglect is our calling to be a citizen of multiple communities—town, state, national, and global communities. Even in a democratic republic, where we have a maximal opportunity to help shape our communities toward Christ, we sometimes don't take advantage of that opportunity. There are many ways that we might miss the opportunity to be responsible Christian citizens. We might err by not taking seriously the responsibility to have an informed and distinctively Christian view on important social and political issues. We might sin by shying away from speaking out about issues when we are in the minority, or, alternatively, by giving our opinions about issues in a disrespectful, unfair, or uncharitable manner. So there are many ways to forsake this responsibility. On the flipside, the fact that God has placed each of us in certain communities provides an awesome responsibility to witness and obey.

First, we can love our communities by faithfully fulfilling our calling to our families, churches, and workplaces. These institutions (family, church, workplace) are the ones that undergird a community and make it a viable place for people to live and flourish. Second, we can love our communities by being active in certain other nongovernmental sectors. We can serve our community's schools and nonprofit organizations. We can help shape public opinion about important issues by engaging in neighborhood and coffee-shop conversations, or by writing in newspapers or blogs, and by doing so in a manner shaped by Christian love and conviction. Third, we can love our community by being actively involved in the political process in ways that reflect true Christian conviction and Christian love.

## Fulfilling Our Callings

Our vocation as Christians is more than a career. God created his imagers to work in multiple spheres. Putting bread on the table is a noble task, but it is just one part of human vocation. Seeing all of life through the lens of vocation helps us see the significance of things we might otherwise consider mundane.

Our callings are our primary means to bring God glory, loving him and our neighbor, and the primary ways in which our lives intersect with various cultural arenas. If we are seeking to fulfill these callings faithfully and with excellence, we will find ourselves able to witness to Christ with the whole of our lives in every dimension of society and culture.

## Action Points

- This chapter identified four callings God gives to his people: family, church, workplace, community. Identify ways that God has called you to love him and your neighbor through these four callings. Be specific.

- These four callings encompass the totality of our lives. We are called to be faithful in our families, churches, workplaces, and communities. Pause for a moment to consider the potential impact on your community if you—and the other members of your church—were to take seriously each of these callings.

- Regardless of context, we run the risk of being out of balance in regards to each area of calling. We can either fall into apathy on one side or idolatry on the other. In what ways have you been out of balance in these spheres? In what ways is this like or unlike the rest of the cultural context in which you live?

## Recommended Reading

DeKoster, Lester, and Stephen Grabill. *Work: The Meaning of Your Life.* 2nd ed. Grand Rapids: Christian's Library Press, 2010. A very short book introducing the Christian understanding of work.

Keller, Timothy. *Every Good Endeavor: Connecting Your Work to God's Work*. New York: Penguin, 2012. A more extensive treatment of the Christian view of work.

Veith, Gene Edward Jr. *God at Work: Your Christian Vocation in All of Life*. Wheaton, IL: Crossway, 2011. A short book introducing the Christian's calling to church, family, workplace, and community.

# CHAPTER 4

# Six Case Studies on Culture

Throughout 2,000 years of Christian history, there are many men and women who lived exemplary lives in their cultural contexts, and from whom we can learn rich and profound lessons. If we overlook these men and women, we do so to our own detriment. For this reason, this chapter will offer six case studies in church history—examples of men and women who sought to direct their cultural activity toward Christ. Although the case studies will be concise to the extreme, I hope to offer lessons that can be learned from each person's life. In this chapter, we will learn about Christians who lived centuries ago, but whose lives are instructive for us in the 21st century.

## Augustine of Hippo

Augustine of Hippo was an early Christian theologian and philosopher who lived during the later years of the Roman

Empire. One of his most famous books was titled *City of God*, and it reveals to us some lessons about Christianity and culture.[1]

Augustine wrote *City of God* just as the Alarics and the Goths were attacking Rome. The Roman intellectuals and common people scrambled to interpret this event, to make sense of it, in much the same way that Americans scrambled to make sense of the 9/11 attack. Many Romans concluded that the real reason for Rome's fall was not the Alarics and the Goths, but the Roman gods, who were taking revenge because the Roman people had embraced Christianity.

As Curtis Chang has noted, the Roman intellectuals' interpretation of Rome's fall was political, religious, and philosophical.[2] It was *political*, arguing that the Romans had abandoned their founding story (Romulus and Remus) in favor of the biblical story of the world. It was also *religious*, arguing that the Romans had abandoned their gods in favor of Christ. Finally, it was *philosophical*, arguing that the Romans had rejected Plato's philosophy in favor of the Christian belief that God came down to earth, took on a human body, and was crucified and rose from the dead so that we could be reconciled to God. On the backdrop of these three arguments, Augustine received a letter from Marcellinus, a Christian who was well known among the culturally powerful and elite, asking for help in answering the Roman intellectuals.

Augustine responded to Marcellinus with a letter that is now published in the form of a 1,000-page book, *City of God*. He argued that the Roman intellectuals' interpretation was wrong, and that all three of their arguments—political, religious, and philosophical—were wrong. Augustine was well prepared to respond to them; he already had taken the time to understand their political, religious, and philosophical beliefs and was able to respond immediately and compellingly.

His basic move was to point out that the Romans were not at the center of the universe. God, through his Son, Christ, is at the center! He showed how the story of Rome's rise to power was really only one small story in the midst of a much larger story of God creating the world and then responding to the world's sin by sending his Son to save us. He explained that Rome (the greatest city in the world at that time) wasn't even an eternal city. There were only two eternal cities, which he called the "city of God" and the "city of man."

Each city has a basic love—either God or idols. Each city is symbolized in the Bible by an earthly city—Jerusalem and Babylon. Each city has a *telos* or end goal—eternal life or eternal death. In making his argument, Augustine not only drew upon his deep knowledge of the Bible and Christian theology, but also used Roman literature, philosophy, politics, and history to make his points. He referred to their great authors and celebrities and quoted them favorably when possible, but he also showed how they fell short of Christian truth.

Significantly, he argued that Rome was an unjust city *politically*. This was a particularly biting argument, because Romans viewed their city as being founded upon just laws.

But Augustine showed that all of their talk about justice and law served only to conceal what they really loved, which was dominating other people. He unmasked their *religious* pretensions, showing that the Romans had never really believed in their gods; even their best religious historians didn't believe in the gods. He unmasked their *philosophical* shortcomings, showing how the deficiencies in Plato's philosophy could be made up for only by Christianity.

What can we learn from Augustine? There are many lessons to be learned, but we will limit our discussion to a few: (1) Augustine was ready when the challenge came. He had spent a lifetime reading and learning, and he was prepared to give a compelling answer when one was needed. (2) He was able to recognize both the good and bad in Roman culture, and to use both the good and the bad aspects to help him point to Christ. (3) He was able to interpret the Bible masterfully *and* interpret his cultural context skillfully. As a result, he could diagnose Rome's disease and use the Bible as a surgeon's scalpel to lay bare the disease for all to see. (4) He wrote *City of God* with such power and beauty that it has become an enduring component of culture. In other words, Augustine was a culture-maker.

## Balthasar Hubmaier

Balthasar Hubmaier was a 16th-century Anabaptist theologian. He preached the gospel under heavy opposition and persecution. One significant moment in his life occurred when he was imprisoned in Zurich in 1525, and under torture

he recanted some of his Christian beliefs. After being re-
leased, Hubmaier repented, confessed his sin of recanting,
and wrote a *Short Apology*—in which he pointed out that he
was human and had erred, but that he would never be a her-
etic because he lashed his theology to the Word of God. A
short while later, in 1528, he and his wife, Elizabeth, were
arrested by authorities, tortured, and tried for heresy. He
was burned at the stake, and she was drowned in the Danube.

Hubmaier is probably best known for his conviction
that Scripture is God's revealed word to humanity, and that
Scripture is the final court of appeal in any theological dis-
pute. He stated this conviction repeatedly, and his life story
supports the weight of his conviction. Both of the imprison-
ments mentioned above came about because of Hubmaier's
biblical convictions.

From Hubmaier we could learn many lessons, foremost
among which are three: (1) Hubmaier, like Augustine before
him, sought for Scripture to shape his cultural engagement.
(2) He was willing to speak his convictions, even in the face
of persecution and martyrdom. (3) In being willing to speak
*against* prevailing cultural winds, he spoke words that were
good *for* his cultural context.

## Abraham Kuyper

Abraham Kuyper lived in the Netherlands in the late 1800s
and early 1900s. He was a pastor, a journalist, a newspaper
founder, a professor, a university founder, a parliament
member, and a prime minister. From these many vantage

points, Kuyper sought to work out the implications of the gospel. Both his writings and his life story show us a Christian who, like Augustine, not only critiqued culture but made culture.[3]

Kuyper is known for his teachings about Christianity and culture, some of the most important of which can be summarized in these nine points:

1. God's creation is good and remains structurally good, even after the fall. This point is significant for a discussion of culture because cultural realities are creational. They stem from God's created humans interacting with this created order.

2. God's creation is a unified diversity, an ordered but multifaceted reality. In particular, God designed the world to have diverse cultural "spheres," such as family life, art, science, church, and business. Each sphere is unique and has God-given principles upon which it is founded. Christians must locate those principles and conform their cultural activities to them.

3. When God told the first couple to have dominion and to work and keep the garden, he was telling them to enhance the good creation he had given them, to bring out its hidden potentials. He was telling them to be culture-makers.

4. In the aftermath of the first couple's sin, all culture-making and cultural interaction is distorted and corrupted by sin.

5. However, God graciously restrained sin and its consequences, keeping it from making the world an unlivable horror. In other words, he enabled people to continue their social and cultural lives.

6. In response to sin, God sent his Son to redeem his imagers and restore his good creation. He has given his Son all authority in heaven and on Earth. Christ is Lord over all creation and therefore Lord over every sphere of culture. We should bring our cultural activity under submission to his lordship.

7. Christians must draw upon God's word and upon their Christian beliefs to guide them in their cultural projects.

8. As we enter the public square to work for the common cultural good, we should use reason and persuasion rather than coercion.

9. When Christians leave the gathering of their churches on Sunday morning, they should do so consciously, seeking to apply their Christian faith to their cultural activities.

I agree with Kuyper's teachings, and each of these nine points serves as a lesson for us today. But in addition to those points summarizing his teaching, here are a few additional lessons gleaned from his life: (1) Kuyper was a savvy and insightful commentator on the culture of his day, knowing his context well enough that he could identify where it was misdirected and corrupted and needed to be redirected toward Christ. He was a skilled interpreter of Scripture, but also a skilled interpreter of his culture. (2) Kuyper was not only a cultural commentator; he was a culture-maker. He founded a university, a church, a political party, and a newspaper and wrote numerous books and articles. (3) Kuyper serves as an example of how we should seek to allow Christ his lordship in every aspect of our lives. Although Kuyper, like the other persons highlighted in this chapter, was an extraordinarily talented person whose life is, in some ways, out of reach for most people, he still serves as an example of the way in which we should try to honor Christ in everything we do and say. For example, we might not have the opportunity to found a university, but we can shape our children's education toward Christ. Similarly, we might never be the leader of our country, but we can vote and interact politically in a way that honors Christ.

## C. S. Lewis

C. S. Lewis was a professor at Oxford and Cambridge during the middle of the 20th century. During his early years, he fought in World War I and was wounded in battle. After returning from war, he became a professor at Oxford University. During his initial years as a professor, he was an agnostic, but he later converted to Christ after extensive conversations with his friend J. R. R. Tolkien. His conversion was dramatic, in the sense that his Christianity affected everything he did. After becoming a believer, he met regularly with Tolkien and other writers to talk about Christianity and literature.

Lewis' conversion was transformative in a way that extended beyond his personal spiritual life and into his career as a writer. He wrote more than 30 books, including science fiction (The Space Trilogy), mythology (*Till We Have Faces*), children's fiction (The Chronicles of Narnia), theology (*Mere Christianity*), and literary studies (*The Discarded Image*). Because Lewis' conversion transformed his worldview, everything he wrote from that point on was affected by his faith. Lewis wrote, "I believe in Christianity as I believe that the Sun has risen, not only because I see it, but because by it I see everything else."[4] In some of the books, such as *Mere Christianity*, Lewis was arguing straightforwardly for his readers to trust in Christ. In other books, such as *Till We Have Faces*, he led his reader toward Christian faith in a more implicit manner, by telling a myth that helps the reader see the beauty of Christianity. In other books, such as his scholarly works including *Allegory of Love* or *The Discarded Image*, the Christian influence was even more subtle.

As Lewis scholar Michael Travers has noted, Lewis viewed evangelism as the main purpose of a Christian's life.[5] Lewis' literary career can be viewed as an extended exercise in evangelism. Not only in his explicitly theological books, but also in his literature, Lewis wanted to translate Christianity into popular language for ordinary people who were not theologians. In his fiction texts, he tried to create in his readers a longing for God, and to help them "see" the gospel in concrete form. He called this type of writing *praeparatione evangelica*, or "preparation for the gospel." So for Lewis, "evangelism" is something that Christians do with their whole lives, not only through interpersonal encounters, but in the work they undertake and the shape of their professional lives.

From Lewis' life and writings, we can learn many things about Christianity and culture, among which are three: (1) Lewis exercised his Christianity in both the professional and popular realms. As scholar and professor, Lewis witnessed to Christ in the scholarly realm by shaping his professional writings and teaching in light of the gospel, but he also witnessed to Christ in the popular realm by writing books that promoted Christ to ordinary people. (2) Lewis recognized the power of fiction to convey truth via his readers' imaginations. Instead of limiting himself to arguments made by logical syllogisms, he often made his arguments through stories and analogies. (3) Lewis expended great effort to communicate Christianity in compelling language, to know how to use words and sentences in the most effective manner for the sake of the gospel.

## Dorothy Sayers

Dorothy L. Sayers was an author, a playwright, a translator of Dante, and an occasional theologian in the first half of the 20th century. During her heyday, Sayers was called the "Queen of Crime" in recognition of her revolutionizing work in the detective-novel genre, work that helped that genre gain legitimacy in literary circles. She had no formal theological training, but she was once offered an honorary doctorate in divinity, which she refused.[6]

Sayers was an Anglican Catholic, more conservative than her father, a country-parish rector. Toward the middle of her career, she got involved with a motorcycle mechanic, who fathered her only child. During this time, her faith was rekindled, and it began to shine through her literary works.[7] Her return to Christianity became apparent, though subdued, in the central character of her crime novels, the religiously skeptical amateur criminologist Lord Peter.

However, for Lord Peter to become a devout Christian would have been out of character, so Sayers pursued other avenues for explicitly Christian culture-making.[8] A significant opportunity arose with a request to write the play for the 1937 Canterbury Festival; it was intended to be a play that accentuated Christian themes, illuminating a doctrine or pericope for the public during the Easter season. The play she wrote for the festival celebrated vocation and service through the arts. For Sayers, vocation was not primarily an economic exercise, but a calling.

Sayers engaged culture as a culture-maker. She was convinced that her work must glorify God by its excellence rather than merely because of explicitly Christian content. During a contract battle over the script of one of her BBC radio dramas—a play about the life of Christ—an editor pleaded with her not to walk away from the contract, writing, "In the writing of these plays the spirit of God would be working through you."[9] Sayers responded:

> I am bound to tell you this—that the writer's
> duty to God is his duty to the work, and that
> he may not submit to any dictate of authori-
> ty which he does not sincerely believe to be to
> the good of the work. ... Above all, he may not
> listen to the specious temptation that suggests
> that God finds his work so indispensable that
> he would rather have it falsified than not have
> it at all.[10]

Doing one's proper job is a most important duty. Subjective demands, such as emotions, must be subordinated to that greater duty. This means that the goal in writing is to express truth. In *Gaudy Night*, Lord Peter convinces Harriet, the novel's protagonist, to rewrite a story because the characters are not fully human and thus the story is not true.[11] In *The Mind of the Maker*, Sayers notes in the preface that the book was not "an expression of personal religious belief."[12] Rather, she was explaining the creeds of Christendom. These theological truths, she wrote, "claim to be statement of fact about the nature of God and the universe."[13] For Sayers, there was, in a very Augustinian way, reality found in the created order. This reality is undeniably, objectively and discernibly true.[14]

Sayers recognized that God reveals aspects of himself through the created order. However, she also recognized the impact of sin on the world as it disrupts the created order, disorders our loves, and distorts our interpretation of God's creational revelation. In other words, since the fall, our culture-making and cultural engagement are corrupted and misdirected, and need to be redirected toward Christ.[15] She saw withdrawing from the culture and becoming one with the culture as twin dangers. The first makes Christianity irrelevant, and the other removes the authentically Christian nature. Sayers' conclusion was that the Church must do the impossible: It must influence culture without becoming identified with the institutions of the culture.[16]

Sayers' literary and theological works are exemplary for several reasons, including these three: (1) Her repeated emphasis on doing work for its own sake illustrates the value of the creation and undermines a dualistic view of the world. (2) Sayers' theological work demonstrates the way in which a layperson with no formal theological training can communicate truth to a wide audience. (3) Sayers points toward the importance of culture and cultural activity while also warning not to be conformed to negative influences. She encouraged attempts to transform culture without being transformed *by* culture.

## Francis Schaeffer

Francis Schaeffer was the director of a Swiss retreat center, L'Abri, and became well known as a teacher and defender of the Christian faith. Schaeffer and his wife, Edith, had moved to Europe to work with a Christian children's ministry, but they ended up founding L'Abri in the village of Huemoz, Switzerland, in a cottage that also served as their home. L'Abri became a place where hundreds and eventually thousands of seekers and skeptics came to have their spiritual and intellectual questions answered.

Schaeffer's daughter Priscilla remembers the excitement she felt as a university student when she realized that her friends at the university were drawn to the Christian faith through interacting with her father. "There wasn't anybody I couldn't bring home," Priscilla said, "no matter how eccentric, how rebellious, how blasphemous. ... I didn't have to be ashamed."[17] The seekers and skeptics who came to L'Abri were ministered to at every level of their humanity—intellectual, social, spiritual. Intellectually, Schaeffer presented Christianity as an all-encompassing world-and-life-view that outstripped all other such views. Socially, seekers took part in meals and evening fellowship with the Schaeffer family and other guests. In terms of their inner spiritual life, they were encouraged to read the Scriptures, pray, and spend time in solitude and reflection.

Notably, the Schaeffers viewed those to whom they ministered as important people who were worthy of time and attention. One L'Abri participant, Dorothy Hurley, remarked:

> When Mr. Schaeffer would talk to you, there was nothing else in the world that was going on. He was totally focused on you and what you were talking about and was very involved, very interested. It wouldn't matter who the person was. It could be from the most simple person to the most intellectual—that focus and interest and involvement was the same. I saw it time

and time again. I experienced it myself, and it wasn't anything false. He was really interested in people, and it was something that was very, very striking. I'd never seen that degree of concentration and having that kind of attention, I don't think, with anybody else.[18]

Schaeffer's biographer, Colin Duriez, summarized his interviews with L'Abri participants by describing Schaeffer's approach as one which was marked by kindness:

His preferred medium was talk—conversation, whether with an individual or with a large group of people. He had the uncanny knack of addressing an individual personally, even if one was sitting with several hundred other people. His tapes, books, and films are best seen as embodiments of his conversation or table talk. The overwhelming impression of those who met him briefly or more extensively, particularly in connection with his homely yet expansive community at L'Abri in Switzerland, was his kindness, a word that constantly occurs in people's memories of him, whether Dutch, English, American, Irish, or other nationality.[19]

As Schaeffer listened to a person's life story and to their questions, doubts, and concerns, he was able to locate common ground with that person and show the ways in which their (non-Christian) worldview was unable to make sense of things for them. Only Christianity can make sense of one's inner life, one's intellectual questions, and of the world at large.

In his efforts to commend Christ, Schaeffer also produced resources. In *How Should We Then Live? The Rise and Decline of Western Culture* (which is a book and a film series), Schaeffer tries to show how the Christian worldview is the only enduringly viable worldview for sustaining a civilization, and how European and American rejections of that worldview were detrimental. In *The God Who Is There*, he argues that God exists and is relevant to human concerns. In *Escape from Reason*, he shows how the rejection of the Christian God causes a person to lose contact with reality and become increasingly irrational. In *Pollution and the Death of Man*, he addresses ecological issues from a Christian point of view. In *A Christian Manifesto*, he provided a Christian response to Karl Marx's *Communist Manifesto* and to the *Humanist Manifesto* of 1973.

From Schaeffer's life and ministry, we learn many lessons, among which are these: (1) Schaeffer expended great effort to understand not only Christianity but also his cultural context. This dual understanding allowed him to be effective as an evangelist and apologist. (2) Schaeffer treated individuals as God's unique creations, made in God's image and likeness. Even when—and especially when—he disagreed with their ideas or actions, he treated them with kindness and respect. (3) Francis and Edith recognized the value of Christian community, so they created an environment in their home that would allow unbelievers to share meals with them, to live life together with Christians, and to otherwise experience Christian love.

## What We Can Learn from History in Order to Live Faithfully Today

Each of us must live faithfully in the time and place where God has put us. This means, on the one hand, that we cannot be slavishly beholden to the past. The ways that Augustine or Lewis made culture and engaged culture will be different from our ways. For Augustine, faithfulness included taking into account Roman gods and Roman politics. For Lewis, it meant bearing witness to Christ in England in the aftermath of war. For us, however, faithfulness must be accomplished in our own 21st-century contexts. On the other hand, we can and should learn from Christians in the past. As we observe the ways in which they proclaimed and promoted Christ in their contexts, we will find instruction for how to do so in our own.

## Action Points

- Augustine argued that Roman civilization was corrupt politically, religiously, and philosophically. Pause for a moment to reflect upon ways in which your own country is corrupt politically, religiously, and philosophically.

- Balthasar Hubmaier was persecuted and eventually killed for his views. How do your Christian views conflict with cultural values? What can we learn from Hubmaier's example as we prepare to face opposition?

- Abraham Kuyper is known for his emphasis on Christ's lordship. What are some facets of your own life and cultural engagement that have not been brought into line with Christ's lordship?

- All the people discussed in this chapter display a creative presence in their cultural context, showing Christ to be Lord of every sphere of life. Who are some people you know to be displaying this same sort of Christ-focused presence?

- Both C. S. Lewis and Francis Schaeffer were known for their ability to listen and meaningfully converse with people. In what ways do you hear those around you? What are the marks of gospel-listening, and how should that influence our gospel-sharing?

## Recommended Reading

Chang, Curtis. *Engaging Unbelief: A Captivating Strategy from Augustine and Aquinas*. Downers Grove, IL: InterVarsity Press, 2000. A brief reflection on the way Augustine and Thomas Aquinas engaged unbelief in their respective cultural contexts.

Duriez, Colin. *Francis Schaeffer: An Authentic Life*. Wheaton, IL: Crossway, 2008. A biography of Francis Schaeffer, written by a man who knew Schaeffer well.

Markos, Louis. *Lewis Agonistes: How C. S. Lewis Can Train Us to Wrestle with the Modern and Postmodern World*. Nashville: B&H, 2003.

An exposition of what Lewis can teach us about engaging with art, science, philosophy, and other realms of culture.

Moore, T. M. *Culture Matters: A Call for Consensus on Christian Cultural Engagement*. Grand Rapids: Brazos, 2007. A helpful introduction to the ways in which some Christians have engaged their respective cultures.

Mouw, Richard J. *Abraham Kuyper: A Short and Personal Introduction*. Grand Rapids: Eerdmans, 2011. An excellent little introduction to Kuyper's life and thought.

# CHAPTER 5

# The Arts

As a young believer and a cultural separatist in the 80s and 90s, I was pretty sure that "the arts" were very bad in some foreboding but non-specific manner. I wasn't sure why the arts were so bad, but it seemed self-evident that I was supposed to be against them, not for them. During my childhood years, I had a rather limited television intake ("The Andy Griffith Show" was an exception, although the presence of Otis made even this show "iffy"), an almost non-existent movie intake (except for Billy Graham movies), and a zero-calorie music diet (classical music and hymns only; rock music was Satan's music, and I knew this because Bill Gothard told me so).

Now, don't get me wrong—I'm happy about the alternatives my parents presented. I read books (lots of them, including biography, history, theology, fiction, etc.), I played sports, and I spent time with my family. But by the time I got to college, I wasn't sure what to do with the arts, including popular art forms like cinema, television, and Top 40 music. I knew that I disagreed with a lot of the messages that were being put forth through those media, but I also knew that some of it was beautiful and that all of it was powerfully influential.

Because of this recognition that I didn't know what to do with the arts, in my college and early seminary years I fluctuated between cultural anorexia and cultural gluttony, sometimes within the span of one week. It wasn't until I met the Christian philosopher L. Russ Bush and read books by Abraham Kuyper, C. S. Lewis, and Francis Schaeffer that I began to learn what to do with the arts. L. Russ Bush was the academic dean and professor of philosophy at Southeastern Baptist Theological Seminary, where I was enrolled. In his introductory philosophy course, he covered the history of philosophy and, while doing so, illustrated by pointing to movies, music, and television shows that espoused particular philosophical viewpoints. In his Ph.D. seminar on "Christian Faith and the Modern Mind," he surveyed late 20th-century art, architecture, cinema, and music, showing the philosophical and religious underpinnings of various artists and works.

During Dr. Bush's courses, he introduced us to Christian art critics such as Hans Rookmaaker (professional art historian and critic) and popular art critics such as Francis Schaeffer (Christian theologian and apologist). Rookmaaker and Schaeffer were friends and influenced each other's work in the realm of art. In this chapter, I will center our discussion on Schaeffer's view of art (which depended in part upon Rookmaaker's) as expressed in his book *Art and the Bible*,[1] because it has some very important things to teach us and because Schaeffer communicates those things in a way that is easily understood by non-professionals in the field of art. Along the way, however, I will add to what Rookmaaker and Schaeffer said, and even express some ideas differently than they might have.

Before we continue, let's define some terms that we will be using and then turn our attention back to the Bible's storyline for a moment. Traditionally the word "art" has been defined as something that imitates the real world (Plato) or as a purposive representation of the world that helps us communicate (Kant). However, the traditional conceptions of art tend to reduce it to one "thing," when there is in fact a myriad of diverse things we recognize as art. The philosopher Nicholas Wolterstorff is onto something when he writes:

> Art plays and is meant to play an enormous diversity of roles in human life. Works of art are instruments by which we perform such diverse actions as praising our great men and expressing our grief, evoking emotion and communicating knowledge. Works of art are objects of such actions as contemplation for the sake of delight. Works of art are accompaniments for such actions as hoeing cotton and rocking infants. Works of art are a background for such actions as eating meals and walking through airports.[2]

In addition to talking about art, we will talk about "artifacts." Artifacts are things made by humans that give evidence of the God-given capacity for creativity, which is part of being created in the image of God. "Artistry" refers to the way humans respond to God's equipping and calling them to be creative.

## The Biblical Storyline

Turning to the biblical storyline, we notice that, in the creation account, God is portrayed as the first artist and craftsman. The world we live in, and we ourselves, are the product of his craftsmanship and artistry. Additionally in those chapters, we learn that he created human beings in his image and likeness—which implies that we will be artful and creative similar to the way God is artful and creative.[3] Good art is art that honors God and causes human beings to flourish. After the fall, however, every dimension of culture, including the arts, has experienced the corrupting and misdirecting influence of sin. Bad art is art that is warped and distorted by sin and idolatry, which arises from a wrong view of God and his good world.

In the midst of this fallen state of affairs, the Son of God came to earth and took on human flesh. He was the exact representation of God (Heb 1:3), the image of the invisible God (Col 1:15). Describing this biblical teaching, a 20th-century theologian named Hans Urs von Balthasar wrote that supreme beauty is the glory of the invisible God radiating in the visible materiality of the world.[4] All art and indeed all culture are measured by the standard of the incarnate Son. Additionally, because of the incarnate Son's redemption, we now seek to bring healing and redirection to the arts, by producing art that honors Christ and is free from the corrupting influence of sin. We do this as an act of *obedience* to Christ and as a *witness* to the world.

## Hans Rookmaaker and Francis Schaeffer

In Rookmaaker's book *Art Needs No Justification*, he makes a good point when he notes that good art does not need to have Bible characters or church content as its subject matter. God made us artfully and wants us to be artful, so the subject matter of the art doesn't matter so much. What matters more is that the art is done from within a Christian worldview, for God's glory, and in a way that helps human beings flourish.[5]

Schaeffer picks up this theme and expands on it in *Art and the Bible*. At the beginning of the book, Schaeffer makes a biblical-theological argument for the goodness of the arts. He begins by arguing for the lordship of Christ over every realm of culture and specifically over the arts. He continues by giving specific examples of Scripture promoting the arts. He hones in on "religious" art and artifacts in the tabernacle and temple, "secular" art in the Bible, Jesus' use of art, the biblical writer's use of poetry and portrayal of music, drama, and dance in the Bible, and finally the pervasively "artful" portrayal of heaven's beauty.

After having built his theological case *for* the value of the arts, he begins to show the reader how to evaluate specific works of art. One of the more noteworthy sections is his provision of four standards by which one can judge a work of art. Although Schaeffer had in mind primarily oil paintings, statues, and similar types of art, the standards he articulates are ones that any Christian can use to evaluate other types of art, such as movies, music, graphic design, or home design.

The first category Schaeffer provides is *technical excellence*. He asks whether a painter's canvas gives evidence of technical excellence in categories such as color, form, balance, the unity of the canvas, its handling of lines, and so forth. Similarly, one could ask whether a movie director is skillful in his use of sound and lighting. The second category he provides is *validity*. In order for a work of art to possess validity, it should have been produced by an artist who is honest to herself and her worldview (or does she, for example, sell out for money?). Does the artist explore themes or questions that are within her depth, or that indicate she is merely trying to impress?

The third category is *content*. Is the artist's worldview resonant with a Christian worldview? A piece of art gives glimpses of an artist's worldview, and an artist's whole body of work will tend to reveal the broad contours of his worldview, even though he may not be aware of this. When a singer sings about love, is his view of love shaped by the biblical teaching about love? When a screenwriter produces a movie script whose theme is the meaning of life, does her treatment of the theme reflect Christianity's deepest teaching on the matter? The fourth category is *integration of content and vehicle*. Does this work of art correlate its content with its style? If the lyrics speak to a theme of personal loss, does the music similarly convey a sense of loss? If the lyrics portray the beauty of romantic love, does the music enhance that sense of beauty or subvert it?

After discussing these four categories for evaluating works of art, Schaeffer distinguishes between four types of artists. His first type, and the one that holds the possibility for art that truly honors God and contributes to the flourishing of humanity, is the *Christian artist who works from within a Christian worldview*. Assuming that this artist is skilled and able to produce art that is technically excellent, valid, and integrated, she will produce the very best sort of art. The second type is *the non-Christian who works from within a consistently non-Christian worldview*, and it serves as the mirror-opposite of the first type. Even if this artist is skilled and able to produce art that satisfies the four categories above, her art will not be the best sort of art and will in some ways subvert God's design for human flourishing.

The third type is *the non-Christian who works with the remnants and residue of a Christian worldview*. This artist does not work consistently from within a non-Christian worldview, but either consciously or unconsciously has adopted elements of a Christian worldview. The fourth type is *the Christian who does not fully grasp the Christian worldview and therefore works with elements of a non-Christian worldview*. This artist is a Christian whose worldview has not been conformed to Christianity and who therefore is not able to produce art that arises consistently from within a Christian view of things. While the first two types are examples of the best-case scenario and the worst-case scenario, the last two types are more of a mixed bag.

Schaeffer was not a professional art critic, and his work has some flaws. However, there is much that a Christian (especially one who is not a professional artist or critic) can learn from him. Building on Schaeffer's ideas above, and modifying them a bit, we can say that: (1) As Christians, we should strive to produce good art—art that arises from within a comprehensive Christian worldview and contributes to the well-being of God's people and of the broader community; (2) good, Christian art does not have to be explicitly religious and often is more powerful when it is not; and (3) as Christians, we should pay careful attention to the art arising from our culture, because it is a significant component of the culture and likely reveals something about the predominant beliefs and lifestyles operating in our context.

## Embracing the Arts

One of the reasons why Christians have been increasingly ineffective witnesses in the United States is that we have neglected our responsibility to glorify God in the arts. I agree with the great writer Dorothy Sayers when she says, "The church has never made up her mind about the Arts, and it is hardly too much to say that she has never tried,"[6] and with the Christian theologian Colin Gunton, who recently wrote, "Christianity has tended to be ambivalent about the arts, at once fostering and developing them and yet always ready to doubt their true value."[7] Christians have paid insufficient attention to this dimension of human culture—a dimension that is significant in God's creation-order and that wields great influence over the hearts and minds of humanity.

We would be foolish to continue minimizing the arts. Abraham Kuyper writes, "Understand that art is no fringe thing that is attached to the garment, and no amusement that is added to life, but a most serious power in our present existence."[8] For this reason, we must accept the challenge recently set forth by the musician and theologian Jeremy Begbie, who wrote, "As the western Churches face the enormous challenge of how the faith 'once delivered' is going to be redelivered in a society increasingly alienated from the institutional Church and increasingly ignorant about the Christian faith, to neglect the arts' potential would be curious, perhaps even irresponsible."[9] Instead of neglecting the arts, we need to encourage our churches to place significance on them and create environments that can produce Christian artists and Christians who engage the arts.

## Action Points

- Art is a key element in our discussion on culture redirected toward God, because few things engage the whole person the way art does. What are some of your favorite expressions of the arts? What brings you joy or elevates your thoughts and emotions to the deeper things of life?

- Name some of your favorite artists (be they musicians, painters, photographers, poets, or novelists).

In which of Schaeffer's four categories of artists would you place them?

- Creating beauty and enjoying beauty are unique to humans in God's creation and are things we are called to do as full-orbed worshipers of God. What are ways that you might use your creative capacities, your artfulness, to enhance your home, workplace, church, or community?

## Recommended Reading

Gallagher, Susan V. and Roger Lundin. *Literature Through the Eyes of Faith*. New York: HarperCollins: 1989. An excellent introduction that shows how reading literature helps us interpret our lives.

Godawa, Brian. *Hollywood Worldviews: Watching Films with Wisdom and Discernment*. 2nd ed. Downers Grove, IL: InterVarsity Press, 2009. An engaging book that equips readers to watch films critically.

O'Connor, Flannery. "The Church and the Fiction Writer" in *Mystery and Manners*, 143–53. New York: Farrar, Straus, and Giroux, 1961. An essay providing insight into the relationship of faith and writing.

Rookmaaker, H. R. *Modern Art and the Death of a Culture*. 2nd ed. Leicester: Inter-Varsity Press, 1973. A modern classic that offers penetrating insight into modern art and the intellectual context beneath it. Advanced.

Schaeffer, Francis A. *Art and the Bible: Two Essays*. Rev. ed. Downers Grove, IL: InterVarsity Press, 2006. A small book encapsulating Schaeffer's approach to the arts.

Seerveld, Calvin. *Bearing Fresh Olive Leaves: Alternative Steps in Understanding Art*. Toronto: Piquant, 2000. An advanced treatment of how Christians can understand, make, perform, and evaluate the arts.

Veith, Gene E. *State of the Arts: From Bezalel to Mapplethorpe*. Wheaton, IL: Crossway, 1991. A useful introduction to understanding the biblical foundations for art and the broad contours of contemporary art.

Wolterstorff, Nicholas. *Art in Action: Toward a Christian Aesthetic*. Grand Rapids: Eerdmans, 1980. A Christian philosophy of art arguing that art has a legitimate and necessary place in everyday life. Advanced.

# CHAPTER 6

# The Sciences

Christians sometimes think that the sciences are somehow at odds with the Christian faith. Perhaps they remember that their biology professor in college was not a Christian, or maybe they have listened to atheists like Richard Dawkins denounce the Christian faith. On top of this, many Christians think of the sciences as being only those disciplines such as physics, chemistry, or biology, and thus think of the sciences as being far removed from ordinary life and from the Christian mission. But in fact, the sciences are not at odds with the Christian faith, and science is not far removed from the Christian life. Although scientists and theologians might find themselves sometimes disagreeing with one another on certain topics, "science" and "Christianity" are never in conflict. In fact, Christianity ought to have a close working relationship with all of the sciences, including not only biology, physics, and chemistry, but also sociology, anthropology, psychology, and medicine.

In this chapter, we will focus our attention on whether the sciences confirm the Christian faith or call it into question. In particular, we will pay attention to a claim made by certain scientists such as Richard Dawkins: that Christianity and science are incompatible and that the modern "scientific" worldview should replace the outdated "Christian" one.

## The Biblical Storyline

Before doing so, however, let's turn our attention back to the Bible's storyline, asking how it can illuminate this chapter's topic. From the creation account, we can infer that God is the first "scientist." He created the universe that scientists study, and he even reveals certain things about himself through our study of the universe (Rom 1:20). God sustains the universe and holds it together (Col 1:15–20) so that it manifests the unity, regularity, and stability that a scientist must demonstrate when studying the world. Additionally, God created humans as inquisitive and rational beings who have both the desire and the ability to study his world scientifically. In a nutshell, science has a unique and powerful capacity to honor God and to cause human beings to flourish.

In the aftermath of the fall, every aspect of creation and culture finds itself corrupted and misdirected by sin. Science is no exception. Scientific investigation is undertaken by fallen human beings who, for example, make an idol out of the sciences by trusting that science can answer life's deepest questions and fix its most perplexing problems. In other words, Westerners often worship science instead of God. Additionally, many Westerners view the story of the modern world as a story in which science has made progress precisely because it has proven Christianity wrong in some of its major teachings. For them, the history of science provides a master narrative of the world—one that they often hold to in a deeply emotional and religious manner. This is one way in which science has been corrupted and misdirected.

Because of the redemption we have in Jesus Christ, we seek to glorify God in every dimension of life and culture, including the scientific dimension. We want to bring healing and redirection to science in those areas where it has been corrupted and misdirected. One way we can do that is by retelling the "story" of science, showing the world that Christian theology and natural science are mutually beneficial dialogue partners. In doing so, we are able to correct the misperceptions that many people have and to help them see God as the enabler and encourager of scientific study.

## The Christian Foundations of Modern Science

One of the first things we should note is the fact that modern science arose within a predominantly Christian civilizational context. At the turn of the 20th century, the French physicist Pierre Duhem began researching the roots of modern science. He concluded that modern science began, in seminal form, in the Middle Ages, and that Christianized Europe was a conducive environment to scientific inquiry.

Nancy Pearcey and Charles Thaxton, in *The Soul of Science*, argue that Duhem was an astute and perceptive observer of the history of science.[1] They note that modern science could have arisen from China or Arabia, as both civilizations had produced a higher level of learning and more advanced technology than European civilization at that time. "Yet," they write, "it was Christianized Europe and not these more advanced cultures that gave birth to modern science as a systematic, self-correcting discipline. The historian is bound to ask why this should be so."[2] Pearcey and Thaxton acknowledge that several factors (e.g., trade and commerce) contributed to Europe's success in the sciences, but they argue that among those factors the Christian worldview was central.

Pearcey and Thaxton list 10 aspects of Christian teaching that enabled modern science to arise in a Christianized European context, several of which we will now mention. One aspect is the biblical teaching that the physical and material world is both real (unlike the illusory world envisioned by many Hindus) and good (contrary to the negative perspective of Gnostics and neo-Platonists). Furthermore, Scripture teaches that the world is good but not divine, which allows humans to study it as an object rather than revering it as a god.

Additionally, the Bible portrays an orderly world that can be studied (unlike the pagans, who viewed the world as a chaotic arena influenced by the conflicting whims of various deities). Its regularity is such that we have come to speak of "the laws of nature," which can be stated in mathematical formulas. Finally, Scripture portrays humans as beings who have the rational capacities to study this orderly world. In other words, God created the world in such a way that it can be studied, and he created humans in such a way that we can do the studying.

Christianity, therefore, played a significant role in the rise of modern science and is hospitable to science and scientists. Not all scientists, however, see it that way. Some of them argue that the claims of science and theology are incompatible—that science trumps theology, and that theology is no longer credible in the modern world.[3]

## Atheism's Errant Claims That Science and Theology Are Incompatible

Stephen Barr is a theoretical particle physicist at the Bartol Institute of the University of Delaware. Several years ago, he wrote an important article in which he showed how there is no real conflict between science and theology. Instead of a conflict between *science* and theology, there is a conflict between *materialism* and theology.[4] (Materialists believe that nothing exists except matter, and they almost always believe there is no God.[5]) Barr argues that Christianity is rational, that it actually gave birth to modern science, and that the Bible's storyline and teachings fit hand-in-glove with the best of science. In the main body of his paper, Barr shows how scientific materialists claim that science makes a Christian conception of the world unbelievable; then he proceeds to overturn each of the materialists' claims. In the next few paragraphs, I will summarize four of the materialists' claims and Barr's response to them.

The first materialist claim is that Copernicus' discoveries overturned Christian cosmology. They argue that Copernicus' discovery that the Earth revolves around the sun refuted a Christian belief that the sun revolves around the Earth. Barr responds that Copernicus did not overthrow any distinctively Christian belief. The earth-centered view of the cosmos came from pagan thinkers (Ptolemy and Aristotle) rather than from Christian Scripture—so Copernicus refuted Ptolemy and Aristotle, not Christianity. Barr goes on to make a very interesting point: Contemporary cosmology has recently moved in the direction of affirming Christian beliefs about the cosmos. While the scientific consensus 30 years ago was that the cosmos was eternal, the consensus now is that it must have had a beginning (which is what theologians have argued for thousands of years).

A second materialist claim is that "mechanism" has triumphed over "teleology." Teleology is the view that the world has a design and a purpose, while mechanism is the view that it does not. Materialists argue that physicists have discovered certain "laws" of physics that hold the world together in such a way that there is no need to believe in a Designer who put it together. Barr argues that this mechanistic view is wrong. Barr is himself a physicist, and he argues that most physicists recognize that deep laws underlie the universe's operations—laws so profound and elegant that they actually cause physicists to postulate some sort of cosmic design. While materialists continue to assert that the universe could not have had a divine Designer, many physicists now suspect that it could or does.

A third materialist claim is that biologists have dethroned humanity from the high position given to it by Christian theology. Materialists say that biology has led us to believe that humans are merely animals who make up just a tiny part of a huge and hostile universe. If this is true, it must disprove Christianity, which teaches that God created human beings in his image and likeness and set them apart from the animals. Barr's response is to argue the opposite point: As it turns out, the universe is amazingly (even gratuitously) hospitable to humans. Many features of our universe are fine-tuned in such a manner that minute alteration would leave the Earth uninhabitable for humans. Such "anthropic coincidences" seem to be built into nature—and if they have been built in, there must be a divine Builder.

A fourth materialist claim is that humans are nothing more than biochemical machines, and that this "fact" renders the God-postulate unnecessary. Materialists argue that there is no proof whatsoever that humans have "souls" or spiritual capacities of any type and that therefore we have no reason to believe in God either. However, Barr explains that some physicists are now arguing that the quantum theory in physics is incompatible with a materialist view of the mind. He concludes that research in physics shows the laws of the universe to be grand and sublime in a way that implies design—and, because of that, this research also implies that the universe has a Designer.

## Science and Theology as Mutually Beneficial Dialogue Partners

The best way to view science and theology is as "mutually beneficial dialogue partners." Like Barr, we recognize that God is the author of both Scripture and nature. If so, then there should be a partnership between those whose primary object of study is Scripture and those whose primary object of study is nature. Theologians and scientists should dialogue with one another and partner together in seeking to understand reality. As philosopher David Clark writes:

> Reality is complex, human knowers access different dimensions of reality using different methods. This is precisely why dialogue among disciplines is important. Dialogue permits us to adopt multiple frames of reference on reality. Still, if *truth* is unified as we hold, we must seek connections between and integration of these multiple frames of reference.[6]

Clark goes on to elucidate some ways that theology speaks to science and science speaks to theology. *Theology speaks to science* by: (1) explaining the origin and destiny of the universe; (2) explaining why it is orderly and can be interpreted; (3) explaining why science matters; (4) helping to guide future scientific research; and (5) helping provide warrant for one scientific theory over another.[7] Moreover, *science speaks to theology* by: (1) offering conceptual frameworks and analogies helpful for elucidating theological concepts; (2) helping provide warrant for one theological interpretation over another; and (3) illustrating and providing further explanation of biblical teaching on aspects of created reality.

The English physicist and theologian John Polkinghorne puts it well when he writes:

The scientific and theological accounts of the world must fit together in a mutually consistent way. In fact, because I also accept the dialogue description of this relationship, I believe that they can do so—not as a mere matter of compatibility, but with a degree of mutual enhancement and enlightenment.[8]

## When Scientists and Theologians Disagree

The discussion of Barr's article raises a question that many Christians have on their mind: How do we find a resolution when certain scientists present evidence that appears to conflict with Christian teaching? As Christians, we believe that there cannot be any real or final conflict between theology and science, because God is the author of both the "book of Scripture" and the "book of nature." If there is a conflict between certain theologians and certain scientists, it exists because of human error in interpreting Scripture or interpreting nature. In other words, there will sometimes be disagreement between theologians and scientists, but there will never be disagreement between God's two books (Scripture and nature).

In light of these convictions, I offer three principles to resolve the disagreements that sometimes exist between theologians and scientists. These three principles are modified from an article written by the Christian philosopher Norman Geisler:

**Either group (theologians or scientists) can err; for that reason, either group should be open to correction.** Both theologians and scientists have made mistakes. On the one hand, centuries ago many theologians thought that the Earth was square, based on biblical texts referring to the "corners" of the Earth. However, scientists have demonstrated beyond doubt that the world is not square, and theologians now realize that the biblical authors used "corners of the Earth" language metaphorically.[9] On the other hand, decades ago many scientists thought the Earth was eternal. However, most scientists now believe in the "Big Bang" theory, which explains that the universe is expanding outward from a point of "infinite density" (which is as close as scientific language can come to saying that it appeared out of nothing).

**The Bible is not a science textbook.** Scripture does make statements that can be investigated and either affirmed or denied by scientists. However, it does not use technical scientific language and it does not give scientific theories. Instead, it uses language that would be accessible to persons who are observing the world from an ordinary human standpoint. When Scripture is interpreted correctly in this manner, we see that God's written Word does not conflict with science in any real or final manner. Any disagreement we find should be located in human interpretive error, rather than in any real conflict between God's two books.

**Science is constantly changing.** One generation of scientists might argue that the universe is eternal, while the very next generation argues that the universe emerged from a point of infinite density and therefore had a beginning. For this reason, Christians should be careful not to hurriedly revise a traditional interpretation of Scripture in order to satisfy the demands of contemporary scientists.

God's revelation of himself gives Christians deep motivation to embrace the sciences and do excellent work in them. Viewed from a Christian perspective, science is the discipline of studying the good world that God has given us. For this reason, we should build into our churches the habit of encouraging those who are gifted to pursue work in the sciences. We should work hard to build world-class research universities that give scientists the freedom to do their work without laying aside their core convictions and the freedom to hypothesize Christianly as they attempt to make sense of the data. Additionally, we should encourage the most gifted and mature of our young people to study science in our Ivy League and major state universities. In so doing, these students will find themselves in places of influence as research scientists or tenured professors of science at those same universities.

## Action Points

- Barr retells the story of science, arguing that science is not in conflict with Christianity. Have you ever encountered a person who thought science and Christianity are in conflict? How would you respond to them if you had the opportunity to do so?

- What are some ways we benefit from science and technology? What are some ways we make an idol out of science and technology?

## Recommended Reading

Behe, Michael J. *Darwin's Black Box: The Biochemical Challenge to Evolution.* New York: Touchstone, 1996. A fetching read by a working biochemist about a central problem with Darwinian theory. The book is technical but accessible to the lay reader.

Carlson, Richard F., ed. *Science and Christianity: Four Views.* Downers Grove, IL: InterVarsity Press, 2000. This book offers four views on the relationship of science and Christianity: Creationism, Independence, Qualified Agreement, and Partnership.

Davis, John Jefferson. *The Frontiers of Science and Faith.* Downers Grove, IL: InterVarsity Press, 2002. A terrific exploration of 10 current scientific issues and their intersection with Christian theology and life.

Keathley, Kenneth D., and Mark F. Rooker, *40 Questions about Creation and Evolution.* Grand Rapids: Kregel, 2014. This is the best one-stop introduction to the contested question of the relationship between creation and evolution.

Pearcey, Nancy R. and Charles B. Thaxton. *The Soul of Science: Christian Faith and Natural Philosophy.* Wheaton, IL: Crossway, 1994. An analysis of the way in which Judaeo-Christian thought funds the scientific enterprise, including a look at mathematics and scientific "revolutions," and the discipline called the "History of Science."

Plantinga, Alvin. *Where the Conflict Really Lies: Science, Religion, and Naturalism.* Oxford: Oxford University Press, 2011. An argument that there is deep resonance between Christianity and science, and deep conflict between atheism and science. Advanced.

# CHAPTER 7

# Politics and the Public Square

As a Christian citizen of the United States, I get the distinct sense that I am living in an increasingly post-Christian country. The majority of Americans no longer consider traditional Christian doctrines (for example, the doctrine of sin) or traditional Christian ethics (for example, biblical sexual morality) to be plausible in the modern world. Christians who do not abandon these beliefs are labeled intolerant and even hateful.

Given the fact that the United States is a democratic republic, the beliefs of the majority affect the lives of the minority socially, culturally, and politically. This reality makes it increasingly important for Christians to figure out the best way to voice their Christian convictions and enact Christian love in the public square. I use the phrase "public square" to refer to our public life—the places where we speak, act, debate, dialogue, and exchange ideas about the best ways to organize our communities, cities, states, and nation.

Certain people—such as politicians, lawyers, and journalists—find that their jobs are inherently oriented to the public square. However, those persons are not the only ones who have the opportunity to participate in the public square. Each of us can be actively involved in shaping public life. As Christians, the question that arises immediately concerns the relationship between our personal religious beliefs and our shared public life: Should we bring our Christianity with us to the public square or should we leave it home?

In this chapter, we will address this significant question about the relationship between religious belief and public life, especially as it pertains to a country like the United States. In the United States, and in many other democracies, Christians find themselves in conversations with citizens who hold very different opinions on the most important matters in public life. In this situation, we must figure out the most appropriate and compelling manner in which to set forth publicly our vision of the good life.

## The Biblical Storyline

In just a moment, we will discuss different views about how to relate religious belief and the public square. But first, let's trace the biblical storyline once again, this time with an eye toward politics and the public square. When we reflect on the biblical account of creation, we realize that Adam and Eve lived in right relationship with God, with each other, and with the created order. This interconnected web of rightly ordered relationships encapsulated God's design for his people to flourish alongside of one another, experiencing harmony and delight in their common life.

After the fall, God's creational design was corrupted and misdirected. In the aftermath of the first couple's sin, humanity experienced broken relationships with God, each other, and the world. Rather than being in loving fellowship with God, we are born predisposed to reject God, competing with him in an attempt to be Lord over his universe. Instead of living in loving fellowship with each other, we experience social brokenness in the form of murder, rape, adultery, ethnocide, slavery, and terrorism, to name a few. Instead of living in perfect mutual reciprocity with God's creation, we treat his creation badly, and his creation supports our life imperfectly. In other words, sin has created a situation in which we need a governing authority to restrict evil and promote the common good (Rom 13:1–5; 1 Pet 2:13–14).

In the West, most countries are governed by some form of democracy, in which "we the people" have a real say in government. We have the opportunity to gather in the public square to discuss and debate matters of concern to the whole society. And yet, because we are finite human beings and sinners, often we do not achieve consensus. We disagree with one another on many of the most important issues in our shared public life, we have difficulty achieving justice for all, and we wage our debates in the most unhelpful and uncivil of manners.

However, because of Christ Jesus' redemption, we find ourselves sent back into the public square in a wholly new way. We have been reconciled to God and seek to live in reconciled relationships with each other and with God's world. We want to put our Christian convictions to work in the political realm, helping to foster justice for our cities, states, and nation. We do these things out of love for the Lord and *obedience* to him. However, we also do it out of love for our fellow citizens and as a *witness* to them. As we employ our Christian love and conviction in the public square, we are providing a preview of a future era when Christ will return and reign as King over a new heavens and earth.

## A Naked Public Square?

We have just now reviewed the biblical storyline, which gives us the broad contours of God's design for our shared human life, sin's corruption of his design, and Christ's redemption that eventually will heal the corruption. Now, we must try to apply these basic truths to a specific question that the Bible does not address directly: How should Christians—who live in a 21st-century democratic republic populated by diverse religions and ideologies, and characterized by political incivility and injustice—act and speak in the public square? More specifically, should we bring our religious beliefs into the public square or should we leave them at home?

One of the foremost American political thinkers of the late 20th century was John Rawls, who taught at Harvard University. His most influential book, *A Theory of Justice*, addresses many of the questions we are asking in this chapter.[1] Rawls argues that American citizens should engage in vigorous public discussion about important political issues but should leave their religious beliefs out of it. He suggests that we hide behind a "veil of ignorance." We should pretend to be ignorant of our own religious convictions (and of other things that could prejudice us, such as our race or socioeconomic class). Rawls thinks that his view will help citizens achieve the most just outcome.

In my view, Rawls' vision for a naked public square is both impossible and unhelpful. All people are religious, and their religion radiates outward into every part of their lives. Rawls' religion was political liberalism, and it deeply influenced his public-square interaction. Our religion is Christianity, and it will—and should—influence our interactions in the public square. As believers, we affirm our Christian convictions as the very things that should help us create a good and just society. We should employ those convictions appropriately as we seek to contribute to the common good.

Many prominent Christian thinkers, such as Richard John Neuhaus, Lesslie Newbigin, and John Howard Yoder, have rejected Rawls' approach in favor of a view that recognizes the need for believers to bring their convictions to the public square. Each of those thinkers offered valuable insights that will prove helpful for Christians who wish to chart a path of Christian faithfulness in our 21st-century context. In the following section, however, we will rely primarily on the insights of Richard Mouw, an American philosopher and theologian who has applied Abraham Kuyper's insights to our contemporary North American context.

## A Convictional Public Square

A core biblical teaching is that all humans are worshipers, either of God or of idols. Our worship is located in the heart, and it radiates outward into all that we do. People who are not Christians are still worshipers, and whatever or whoever they worship radiates outward into all that they do, including their public-square interactions. As Christian believers, we worship the God of Jesus Christ. Because he is the creator and Lord of all that exists, we seek to bring all of our lives, including our public-square interactions, into submission to his lordship. The question remains, however: "How exactly do we bring our public-square interactions in line with Christ's lordship?" Here are seven points that offer a way forward.

### 1. We want to avoid a coercive relationship between the church and the state.

From Genesis, we learn that God created the world and ordered it by means of his world. This ordering includes various spheres, such as family, church, art, science, and politics. Each sphere has its own creational design, its own way of reflecting God's glory and enabling humans to flourish. Ideally, each sphere exists directly under God's lordship, rather than under the "lordship" of one of the other spheres. For example, the church should not seek the authority of the state, and the state should not encroach upon the church.

On the one hand, we should avoid "ecclesiasticism"—a situation in which the church seeks to control the state. There are many instances in history in which the institutional church has sought to exercise power directly over the government. However, Scripture never directs or encourages the church to do so. Although God himself is sovereign over the government and can exercise authority directly over it, the church is not sovereign in this manner. Instead, the church is called to equip its members to live godly lives and to be salt and light in their public-square interactions.

On the other hand, we must avoid "statism"—a situation in which the state encroaches upon the other spheres and especially (for our purposes) upon the church. As Roger Williams, John Locke, and others argued so compellingly in years past, the Christian doctrine of the image of God implies religious freedom. Os Guinness writes, "Freedom of religion and belief affirms the dignity, worth and agency of every human person by freeing us to align 'who we understand ourselves to be' with 'what we believe ultimately is,' and then to think, live, speak and act in line with those convictions."[2] Just as the individual person possesses freedom of conscience, so societies should provide a freedom of religion in the public square.

Although the state should not encroach upon other spheres, and especially not upon the church, this does not mean that the government cannot interfere in these autonomous spheres. Mouw follows Kuyper in noting three such instances. The government of any country can and should play the role of a referee when there is conflict between the spheres (e.g., it might restrict an artist from displaying obscene art in public). It can protect the weak from the strong within a given sphere (e.g., it might interfere in a family after an instance of abuse). It also can use its power in matters that affect multiple spheres (e.g., it taxes us in order to build roads that enable all spheres to function).[3] Finally, I add that a government ideally will create an environment in which all of the spheres can operate healthily, enabling society to flourish.

## 2. We should be active in promoting the common good.

In Romans 13:1–7 Paul urges the Roman church to live in submission to its government. However, this passage cannot be employed to justify ultimate allegiance to the government or a passive citizenship in contemporary democratic situations. As Mouw explains:

> In modern democracies, the power of national leaders is derived from the populace, which is the primary locus of God-given authority. Built into the very process is the possibility of review, debate, reexamination, election, and defeat. Given such a framework, for Christians simply to acquiesce in a present policy is to *fail to respect* the governing authorities.[4]

God has always called his people to be a light to the nations, and contemporary democracies provide a unique venue for being just such a light. We can be salt and light not only by calling people to salvation, but also by promoting the common good and looking for ways to restrain public evil.

### 3. We should be discerning in how we articulate our beliefs.

As we are looking for ways to promote the common good and restrain sin and its effects, we will have to provide a rationale for the ways we suggest. When providing a public rationale, we face a choice between articulating that rationale in explicitly Christian language or with more neutral language. If we give a more robust and explicitly Christian rationale for our proposals, we often run the risk of being ignored or misunderstood. If we give a more neutral rationale, we are not able to speak with the same convictional force or precision. For example, if a Christian is arguing against abortion, she might in one instance articulate her rationale in terms of the Christian doctrine of the image of God, but in another instance focus on demonstrating the negative effects of abortion on families and the broader society. Such choices are difficult, and we must pray for wisdom and discernment about the best way to argue our points.[5]

### 4. We should be discerning in what we say from our pulpits.

The gospel we preach is political (we declare that Jesus is Lord and "Caesar" is not), and therefore the church is a political community. We are political in the sense that we are a "contrast community" whose life is ordered under Christ and should be markedly different from other communities. Our power does not come from wealth, social position, or military power. Instead it comes from Christian love, prophetic witness, generosity, and sacrificial service.

One contested issue is whether politics should be preached from the pulpit. This is not an easy question. Mouw is right when he says that we should proceed carefully and pray for discernment when faced with the question of whether to address a political issue from the pulpit. If we decide to do so, we must be confident that our words and concerns arise from God's words and concerns as expressed in Scripture. If we are confident that our words and concerns match God's, we might address the situation directly.[6] If we are not so confident, we might merely raise a question about the issue and say that Christians should pray for discernment. A preacher might be confident in addressing the evil of abortion from the pulpit, for example, but likely would not preach about federal regulation of the aviation industry.

### 5. We should be civil in our demeanor.

Public square interactions often become contentious, and Christians should make sure that their interactions are shaped by their love for Christ and for their fellow humans. We should be courteous toward those with whom we disagree. We should represent our debate partners accurately rather than misrepresenting them. We should recognize the good in their lives and their arguments, rather than glorifying ourselves and demonizing them. We should be teachable, rather than close-minded. In a nutshell, we should be publicly righteous and our churches should be formation centers for public righteousness.[7]

## 6. We should be realistic in what we expect from the political sphere.

As believers, we should be measured in what we expect from the political realm. After all, we are sinners, our politicians are sinners, and in fact we live in societies full of sinners. However, we also know that Christ Jesus will return to institute a new order in which righteousness will prevail. So we should be neither pessimists who throw up our hands in despair nor utopians who try to force the present era to be the new heavens and earth. Instead, we should be clear-eyed Christian realists, who participate patiently in the public square, seeking to bear witness to Christ and promote the common good.

## 7. We should remember that politics is only one dimension of our cultural witness.

Before concluding our discussion of religion and the public square, I think it is important to remind ourselves that politics is only one dimension of culture. Additionally, what happens in the political realm often is influenced by things that have taken place in other realms. In other words, if we want to influence our society, we should not put all of our hopes in politics. We should expend our energies in *all* arenas of culture, because each of those arenas affects what happens in the political realm. Consider the influence that universities have in shaping the minds and hearts of young men and women. Or consider the power of the arts (especially music, TV, and movies) to shape the way entire cultures and subcultures think and feel about issues. So politics is one arena among many, and it is shaped by the other arenas.

## Grace and Joy in Politics

As Christians, we should participate in politics and in discussions about the public good. We do so with seriousness, because Christian love and conviction demand that we work for the public good. We do so with grace, because Christian love extends even to people with whom we have irreconcilable differences politically. And we do so with joy, because our final hope is in Jesus Christ, rather than in the United States of America.

## Action Points

- Reflect on incivility in public life. Can you think of current examples of Christians who interact in public life in ways that are uncivil, such as misrepresenting or demonizing those on the other side of a political debate?

- Pick a public-square issue (e.g., just war, abortion, health care). How would you address this issue if you were invited to speak about it on national television? Would you give an explicitly Christian rationale for your stance, or would you choose to use more neutral language? What type of tone would you use?

- Christianity is political in the deepest sense of that word. Jesus is Lord, and Caesar is not. However, preachers should be cautious about addressing political issues from the pulpit. Identify appropriate and inappropriate instances of addressing political issues from the pulpit.

- When we are unrealistic about what we expect from politics in a fallen world, we can become angry, depressed, and cynical. Can you think of ways in which you or others are unrealistic in your expectations?

## Recommended Reading

Audi, Robert and Nicholas Wolterstorff. *Religion in the Public Square: The Place of Religious Convictions in Public Debate.* Lanham, MD: Rowman & Littlefield, 1997. A somewhat technical discussion of Christian convictions and the ways in which believers should dialogue in the public square. Audi argues that Christians should appear "naked" in the public square, while Wolterstorff (himself a political liberal), argues that they should come "fully clothed."

Budziszewski, J. *Evangelicals in the Public Square: Four Formative Voices on Political Thought and Action.* Grand Rapids: Baker Academic, 2006. This intermediate-to-advanced book describes the way four theologians—Carl Henry, Abraham Kuyper, Francis Schaeffer, and John Howard Yoder—approached the public square.

Mouw, Richard J. and Sander Griffioen. *Pluralisms and Horizons: An Essay in Christian Public Philosophy.* Grand Rapids: Eerdmans,

1993. An unpacking of the problem of political consensus in a pluralist environment, which includes a helpful comparison and contrast of major thinkers on the topic, including John Rawls, Robert Nozick, and Richard John Neuhaus.

Mouw, Richard J. *Uncommon Decency: Christian Civility in an Uncivil World*. 2nd ed. Downers Grove, IL: InterVarsity Press, 2010. An argument that Christians should bring not only their Christian convictions to the public square, but also their Christian virtue—especially the ability to be civil in the midst of debate and discussion.

Neuhaus, Richard John. *The Naked Public Square: Religion and Democracy in America*. Grand Rapids: Eerdmans, 1984. A very influential and well-argued text on the place of Christian conviction in public political discourse.

# CHAPTER 8

# Economics and Wealth

In the previous chapter, we discussed the relationship of Christian religious beliefs, politics, and the public square. In this chapter, we will discuss an issue at the center of many political discussions and debates: economics and wealth. Does the Bible have anything to say about this topic? We will see that the Bible does, in fact, provide some guidelines for Christians who want to manage their personal wealth in the right way and who want to live in a society that is economically healthy and just.

Matters of economics and wealth are important to us not only because they affect our livelihood, but because Jesus spoke about them often. The broader economy either enables or disables us in our attempts to flourish and prosper. In one way or another, it affects all of our callings (family, church, workplace, community) and every arena of culture (art, science, business, education). Our view of wealth, and our possession of it, likewise affects all of our callings and can affect our interactions in the broader culture.

As in previous chapters, this topic is too broad to cover in such a short chapter, even if I tried to cover just the basics. For that reason, I will once again focus on a single aspect of our topic that is relevant to Americans in the 21st century: Marxist socialism. During the 20th century, the nations of the world clashed over Marxism—and in many ways, even today, any discussion of economics is affected by it. I will provide a brief description of Karl Marx's views and then show how they tend to undermine biblical wisdom concerning the economic realm. Then, I will argue that a healthy brand of capitalism fits well with biblical teaching. But before doing so, let's trace the biblical storyline in order to see what it has to say about wealth and the economy.

## The Biblical Storyline

In the beginning, God's creation was one in which Adam and Eve could flourish in the midst of created abundance. God told them to "have dominion" over (manage) this world of abundance, and to "till the soil" (bring out the hidden potentials) of this abundant world. At the time of creation, there were no wealth-related sins such as theft or greed.

After the fall, however, things changed dramatically. In the chapters and books immediately following the story of the first couple's sin, we notice humans sinning in their *acquisition* of wealth. Instead of working to acquire life's necessities and luxuries, they stole from others. For this reason, the eighth commandment says, "You shall not steal" (Exod 20:15), and the writer of Proverbs praises hard work while criticizing laziness (Prov 6:6–11). People also sinned in their *use* of wealth. For this reason, the Bible commends those who share with others rather than hoarding for themselves (Acts 2:44-45) and who pay a fair wage to those who work (Acts 5:3-4). Finally, people also sinned in their *view* of wealth and possessions, by seeing those things as ultimate rather than seeing God as ultimate. For this reason, we are warned to not make an idol out of silver (Eccl 5:10) or earthly treasures (Matt 6:19-24), to not be greedy (Prov 28:25), and to not be anxious about the material things that we need (Matt 6:25-34).

Because of Christ's redemption, we have been set free to redirect our lives wholly toward Christ, and this redirection includes the economic aspect of our lives. In terms of the *acquisition* of our wealth, we want to work hard to earn the things we need and want, and to make sure that our labor is always done morally and legally. In terms of the *use* of our wealth, we should view our possessions as being (ultimately) God's possessions and have an attitude of thankfulness toward God, who is the provider of those things. We should be generous to those who have need, especially those (such as widows and orphans) who are least able to provide for themselves. We should not allow wealth to cause divisions within the church, and we should not display favoritism toward the wealthy. In terms of our *view* of wealth and possessions, we should never treat those things as ultimate or as saviors, because only God is ultimate and only he can save.

## Karl Marx and Socialism

The field of economics is beyond our ability to summarize in this chapter, so, again, I will select one aspect of the topic that will be helpful and interesting for most people reading this book. Our chosen topic is Karl Marx and his view of economics and wealth, which is a certain brand of socialism. Marx is the thinker behind the communist revolutions of the 20th century, and in some ways he is the shaping hand behind socialist economies in the 21st century.

Marx believed that economic factors are the most important factors in any society and culture. He argued that world history is really a history of people struggling with economic reality and treating each other well or badly based on that reality. In their famous book, *The Communist Manifesto*, Marx and Friedrich Engels wrote, "The history of all hitherto existing society is the history of class struggles, [contests between] freeman and slave, patrician and plebeian, lord and serf, guild-master and journeyman, in a word, oppressor and oppressed."[1] Marx believed that humanity had evolved in stages economically—from hunter-gatherer societies, to slave-based societies, to medieval feudalism, to modern capitalism. And in his mind, capitalism needed to evolve into socialism.

Marx criticized capitalism by arguing that it undermines national identities and cultural distinctives, because it encourages people to clamor for wealth rather than honoring those traditional identities and distinctives. Most important, he argued that capitalism dehumanizes people by alienating them from their labor. In his view, capitalist economies value money and wealth acquisition more than they value workers. They view the worker as a business expense rather than as a human being. And, judging from the state of capitalism today, Marx's critique has some truth to it. But his solution was extreme: He believed that workers of the world should (and would) overthrow capitalism.[2] When that happened, he argued, workers should abolish private property and eventually abolish the state itself.

It is important to note that socialism is a broad category, and Marxism is just one version of it. To make things even more complex, Marx viewed socialism as only a temporary stage on the way to an even better (in his view) economic system: communism. Marx envisioned a day when his socialism (with state ownership of property) would be replaced by communism (in which the state would no longer exist). Marx's wishes were never fulfilled. In fact, quite the opposite happened: Marxist socialism has always created an even bigger and more intrusive government than existed before.

## The Problem with Marxist Socialism

One criticism of Marxist socialism is that it wants to abolish private property. But the ownership of private property is closely tied to freedom and liberty, which are essential to God's design for human culture. When the government takes public ownership of all property, it reduces our ability to interact freely with each other in every cultural arena.

Another criticism of socialism is based on the work of an economist named Ludwig von Mises, who argued that economic activity isn't sustainable without pricing set by the free market.[3] Take, for example, the Soviet version of Marxist socialism. In its centrally planned economy, the prices were not determined naturally by supply and demand (as they are in capitalism), but instead were determined artificially by the government. Officials in Moscow set prices on goods and services all around the country, from eggs to tractors to heart surgeries. The problem with this approach is that it severely reduces the incentives people have to do their work with creativity and excellence, because there is no financial reward for it. If heart surgeons get paid the same as street sweepers, then the men and women who have the potential to make breakthrough discoveries in heart surgery might never have the motivation to go through many years of medical school or to work the 60–70 hours per week that world-renowned heart surgeons work. When there is no incentive for progress, the culture stagnates or declines.

A final criticism, and a very serious one, is that socialist forms of government have to be more coercive than democratic capitalist forms. The more the government controls, the more power it has. The 20th-century Russian version of socialism was authoritarian, as are the ongoing systems in Cuba and China.

## A Christian's Argument for Capitalism

Capitalism is a form of economy that values a free market rather than a restricted market. Capitalists believe that value arises naturally from supply and demand, rather than artificially by the hand of the government. If the rule of law is in place, and if the economy is undergirded by an overall moral citizenry, then the prices of goods will tend to reflect the underlying supply and demand. Capitalists want citizens to own property and workers to receive the monetary reward for hard work, creativity, and excellence in their labors. In a nutshell, they believe that a free market is the economic system for helping people to flourish in a fallen world.

The Bible does not actually set forth a preferred economic system paired with a preferred system of government, so we have to be creative in trying to figure out which type of economic and political system best fits biblical principles. A Christian thinker named Michael Novak wrote an important book, *The Spirit of Democratic Capitalism*, in which he argued that biblical principles can be honored best in a democratic capitalist system.[4]

One of Novak's arguments in favor of capitalism is that the free market encourages competition, which in turn provides incentive for people to build better businesses and create better products and services. This sort of economic progress, if it is accompanied by a moral citizenry, will provide all sorts of benefits to a society. The better the products and services we provide for one another, the more likely we are to flourish. God will not judge us for creating wealth, but for our use of it. He blesses us so that we can bless others.

Another of Novak's arguments is that the Bible encourages us to build societies that respect the realities of a fallen world. Marxism does not do that; it seeks to create a utopia, a human version of the kingdom of God. But capitalism recognizes, for example, that fallen people generally need economic incentives in order to do their best work.

Novak's argument for free-market capitalism is much broader and deeper than what I've described, but those two arguments are examples of how we can apply biblical principles to economic realities.

## Misdirected Capitalism

Yet, even though free-market capitalism is our preferred economic system, it can be corrupted and misdirected. In *Two Cheers for Capitalism,* Irving Kristol rightly cautions free-market proponents not to be so enthusiastic for capitalism that they self-destruct. In our support for the free market, therefore, we must be wary of potentially destructive misdirections.

One way we can misdirect the free market is by idolizing the goods and services offered by the market. The free market does not itself make judgments on what people buy or how much they buy. People can buy (almost) anything they wish, as long as they can pay for it. In allowing that type of liberty, the free market opens the door to materialism and consumerism. Materialism is the belief that we will be happier if we acquire more goods and services, while consumerism is our preoccupation with acquiring those goods and services. The materialist-consumerist mindset is idolatrous, because consumption becomes a functional savior offering the sort of redemption that only Christ can offer, and promoting the sort of utopia that will exist only in the new heavens and earth. Not only individuals but also entire societies can make an idol out of the consumption of material goods and services.

Another way we can misdirect the free market is by fostering an unhealthy relationship between the government and large corporations, a relationship we can call "cronyism" or "corporatism." In cronyism, the government uses regulators to control corporations. Significantly, and to the detriment of a free market, many of the regulators work in the very offices of those corporations, as if the regulators were actually now a part of the corporation. Government officials can be attracted to this model because they are able to control the corporation. If things go bad, the government can blame the corporation, but if things go well, the government can claim credit. Large corporations can be attracted to this model also, because they are able to collude with the government to prevent competition and to protect themselves.

In addition, in the United States there are strategically important financial institutions so critical to our economy that they are protected by the government. The government "gives" to these institutions by protecting them financially in such a way that they cannot fail, but in return "takes" from them the regulation of their own business. Alexis de Tocqueville predicted this approach in the 18th century and called it "soft tyranny."

Because we do not have the space to go into greater detail in this little book, let's summarize crony capitalism by saying that it exerts too strong a control over free enterprise.[5] An optimal free market is one that keeps government from controlling businesses and encourages healthy competition between businesses, which in turn incentivizes businesses to create better products and services. This free-market environment, if it is supported by a moral citizenry, will provide the optimal environment for its citizens to flourish.

## Security in God, not Wealth

The Bible does not prescribe for us any particular economic system or any particular form of government, and it certainly does not prescribe for us the way in which economic systems and forms of government should fit together. But we have tried to argue that a democratic capitalist form of government can be a very healthy way of applying biblical principles, especially if the citizens of that nation are moral, and if they resist the excesses of materialism and consumerism.

Christians who live in a democratic capitalist society are in a unique position to be able to elect representatives and have a voice in the economic direction of our nations. We should take seriously our responsibility to vote and to voice our opinion in the public square. But even closer to home is our responsibility to acquire, use, and view our personal wealth in a way that pleases God. We should work hard to acquire our wealth in a way that is moral, legal, and beneficial to society. We should use the wealth we possess to bless our families, but also to bless our neighbors. We should never lose sight of the fact that God, rather than wealth, is our security and our savior.

## Action Points

- What are some biblical truths that our 21st-century societies need to hear regarding the economy?

- Do you sometimes find yourself slipping into a materialist or consumerist mindset? What goods and services seem to trigger this for you? How can Christians resist the excesses of materialism?

- What are ways that you can begin living as a preview of God's kingdom in relation to economic realities? How do you live out obedience and faithful witness in this realm of life?

- Imagine a scenario in which you find yourself in a public disagreement about an economic issue. The person you are disagreeing with is a member of a different political party. Keeping in mind what we learned in the previous chapter about grace, joy, and civility, how should you interact with this person? What should be your tone? How closely would you associate your opinions with your Christianity?

## Recommended Reading

Brand, Chad. *Flourishing Faith: A Baptist Primer on Work, Economics, and Civic Stewardship*. Grand Rapids: Christian's Library Press, 2012. This book is the most concise and accessible primer I know of that addresses work, economics, and civic stewardship.

Corbett, Steve and Brian Fikkert. *When Helping Hurts, How to Alleviate Poverty Without Hurting the Poor... and Yourself*. Chicago: Moody, 2014. The authors lay a foundation for social ministry and poverty-alleviation by defining Jesus' gospel and mission. From there, they show how social ministry and poverty-alleviation can be accomplished without hurting the poor or hurting the church.

Grudem, Wayne. *Business for the Glory of God.* Wheaton, IL: Crossway, 2003. A short introduction to the Bible's teaching on the moral goodness of business and entrepreneurship.

Novak, Michael. *The Spirit of Democratic Capitalism.* Lanham, MD: Madison, 1991. A vigorous examination of capitalism and democracy with a particularly good articulation of a "theology of democratic capitalism."

Richards, Jay W. *Money, Greed, and God: Why Capitalism Is the Solution and Not the Problem.* New York: HarperCollins, 2009. An excellent argument that Christians can and should work from within the free-market economy (rather than viewing it as evil) to help our world flourish.

———. *Infiltrated: How to Stop the Insiders and Activists Who Are Exploiting the Financial Crisis to Control Our Lives and Our Fortunes.* New York: McGraw Hill, 2013. A deft exposé of big-government economic regulation and the crippling effects of cronyism.

# CHAPTER 9

# Scholarship and Education

When an 18-year-old believer enters college, she often is entering an environment in which the smartest people she will meet (her professors) are opposed to Christianity. In fact, many universities and academic disciplines have become breeding grounds for professors who take delight in undermining or even mocking our deepest Christian convictions. The university is one of the most influential institutions in the modern world, a funnel though which hundreds of thousands of young people pour out annually into every sector of American life. It is not altogether implausible to say, "As goes the university, so goes the next generation."

As Christians, we should expect to encounter resistance from the world. In fact, Jesus promised his disciples that they would be persecuted (John 15:20). However, from my experience, I've learned that many 18-year-olds enter college with very little ability to think Christianly or critically. For that reason, instead of being able to enter into serious discussion and debate, they either compartmentalize their faith or compromise their convictions. When a student "compartmentalizes" his faith, I mean that he tends to dissociate his Christian belief from his academic learning, as if the two didn't have anything to do with each other.

Compartmentalization is one way a student can resolve the tension when his professor's teaching contradicts Christianity. Another way to resolve the tension is to compromise one's convictions. In this scenario, the student doesn't know how to respond to views that conflict with a Christian worldview, and so he chooses the professor's views over his Christian worldview.

This sort of scenario is quite common. The intellectual environment in the United States is one in which non-Christian worldviews are privileged. In particular, "secular" forms of thinking are privileged. Trinity International University's President David Dockery writes:

> The 'cultured despisers' of religion regard faith, Christian faith in particular, as irrational and obscurantist. They consider that it may be necessary to tolerate and perhaps even accommodate faith on campus by providing or recognizing denominational chaplaincies, student religious groups, and so forth. But religious faith, even when tolerated, is understood as at best irrelevant to, and at worst incompatible with, serious and unfettered intellectual inquiry and the transmission of knowledge to students.[1]

However, as Christians, we believe that Jesus Christ is the creator and savior of the world, and that the Bible's teachings about the world are true and trustworthy. For this reason, we should allow our Christian convictions to motivate our learning and to shape it.

The world of education is multifaceted and broad. In this chapter, we will focus in on one aspect of the world of education: Christians who find themselves in a college or university environment. We will discuss how Christians can approach higher education in a way that honors God and produces excellence in learning. Before doing so, however, we need to review the broad contours of the biblical storyline to glean some basic insights about education.

## The Biblical Storyline

The world that is studied and taught about in any school or university is in fact God's creation. When God created the heavens and earth, he was creating the very world that we examine in a math or science course. He was shaping the men and women about which we study when we take classes in psychology, English, or marketing. Additionally, he is the one who gifted human beings with the ability to teach and study; he is the one who endowed us with physical, intellectual, creative, moral, spiritual, and relational capacities.

After the fall, however, we know that human beings experience difficulty in their ability to learn. The Apostle Paul argues that our ability to discern the truth about reality is warped and corrupted by the sin and rebellion present in our hearts. For this reason, when we receive the redemption offered by Christ Jesus, we must allow him to redirect our minds toward him, so that we can allow him and his Word to shape our learning. God's Word serves as an enabling Word, which motivates us to learn and shapes the way we learn. In this way, our teaching and learning become forms of *obedience* and *witness*. We conform our thinking to Christ who is the Lord of all teaching and learning, and we witness to others by allowing our educational *words* and *deeds* to point to him.

## God's Design for Education

Many different proposals have been made about how to build schools and universities that are distinctively Christian. The best of those proposals are the ones that recognize that the Christian worldview not only motivates us to teach and learn, but also shapes the way we teach and learn. A truly Christian education is one which is holistic; in other words, it shapes, in one way or another, every academic discipline, every professor, and every student in a university.

The Bible's basic storyline provides a framework for understanding reality. In a Christian university, that framework influences the way each discipline is taught. Because God created the world, we know that there is a design and order inherent to it, so that it can be studied; based on this, we also know that in each discipline there is a way things ought to be. Because humans are fallen, we know that every academic discipline can be corrupted and misdirected and therefore should be redemptively redirected toward its proper end. Most important, because God is creator of the whole world about which we teach and study, the whole world possesses a certain unity. All things were created by God and are held together by God. The implication for Christian universities is that the curricula and courses should be taught in such a way that the student can comprehend the unity of truth. Each academic subject and each course should be placed in the context of the broader body of knowledge that finds its unity in Christ.

## The Sinful Misdirection of God's Creation

One of the reasons we find it so difficult to build truly Christian universities is that universities in the United States and Europe have tended to sideline religious belief. For several hundred years now, our state universities and most of our private universities have encouraged professors to keep their religious beliefs private. In other words, university education has been marked by the dis-integration of religion and education, rather than the integration of them.

This disintegration caused a Christian historian named George Marsden to write a book, *The Outrageous Idea of Christian Scholarship*, in which he argues that truly Christian scholarship is rare because Christian scholars have been trained to keep their religious beliefs private. He quotes a political scientist named John Green, who said:

> If a professor talks about studying something from a Marxist point of view, others might disagree but not dismiss the notion. But if a professor proposed to study something from a Catholic or Protestant point of view, it would

> be treated like proposing something from a
> Martian point of view.[2]

Marsden argues that American universities tend to force their professors to be quiet about their faith if they want to be accepted at the university.[3]

This sort of disintegration warps and stunts the process of teaching and learning. Historically, the earliest medieval universities and many of the modern universities were truly uni-versities because they understood knowledge to be unified—that is, they saw God as the creator of everything that they studied and taught. However, once modern universities began to sideline religious belief, universities slowly became dis-universities, because God could no longer serve as the center that allowed the disciplines to be unified.

This sort of disintegration has fostered negative developments in education, such as relativism and scientism. Once the universities no longer had a centering point (God) around which knowledge could be unified, it was easy for that disunity to turn into *relativism*. In the faculty lounges and classrooms of many universities today, an atmosphere of intellectual and moral relativism reigns. Alternately, the decentering of God caused a tendency toward *scientism*. If God has been sidelined, then his revealed word has been sidelined, as well. And if this religious perspective is sidelined, then it is easy to think that the scientific perspective on reality is the only perspective. So instead of viewing science and theology as mutually beneficial dialogue partners (see chapter 6), and instead of recognizing the spiritual dimension of human life, the modern world tends to view science as the supreme (or only) form of knowledge and as the ultimate cultural authority.

In response to disintegration, relativism, scientism, and other ills, Christian universities, professors, and students need to bring their Christian worldview to bear upon their teaching and learning. We don't want to merely tack onto the lectures some Bible verses or a prayer, but to do the hard work of figuring out how God's revealed word applies to the subject we are teaching or learning. We cannot be simplistic about Christian education. The way in which Christianity applies will differ according to the subject being studied, and often it will be hard to discern.

In the instance of moral philosophy or ethics, we can fairly readily understand the way that biblical teaching speaks to the subject matter at hand. The Bible contains a significant amount of straightforward teaching on ethics and morality. Similarly, it might be easy to see the way biblical teaching informs a literature course. When an English class studies a novel, for example, students can fairly readily see how the story-world created by the author is a world that makes judgments about life's meaning and purpose, or about truth, goodness, or beauty.

However, there are other subjects in which the Christian application might not be so easy to discern. Take, for example, a course in veterinary studies. And take, for further example, the fairly superficial subject of "how to properly wash a cat"—which can serve as a scenario we might find very difficult to relate to the Christian worldview. How in the world would a Christian worldview shape the way a person teaches about feline hygiene? We can begin by noting that (1) the doctrine of creation reveals that the animal world is part of God's good creation, and therefore animals are not inherently evil. For this reason, an ethical treatment of animals leads us to avoid cruelty toward them. In addition, (2) the doctrine of creation makes clear that animals, including cats, are not created in the image and likeness of God; only humans are. For this reason, one should not wash one's cat with more care than one washes, say, one's baby. Humor aside, society should not value animal life more than it values human life. It should not craft policies against animal cruelty while at the same time allowing human babies to be exterminated before birth. (3) From the doctrine of the kingdom, we know that God will one day restore and renew his good cosmos (Rom 8:18–22; Rev 21–22), including animals. Therefore our care for animals is in some way a preview of God's coming kingdom, in which, the Bible tells us, lambs and wolves will lie down together (Isa 11:6; 65:25). Therefore, (4) we conclude that we should behave responsibly toward cats (Christian worldview) and refrain from worshiping them (as do certain ancient and Eastern worldviews) or being cruel to them (classic middle-school-boy worldview).

Building truly Christian learning environments will be difficult because we must operate simultaneously within two traditions (Western and Christian). We certainly can learn from the Western tradition, but we also will always be at odds with it, because it sidelines religious belief and therefore warps and distorts knowledge. Craig Bartholomew and Michael Goheen put it well when they write, "On the one hand, since God is faithful to his creation, much true insight into God's world will come to us from the non-Christian academic community; on the other hand, the idolatry that underlies Western scholarship will be at work to distort that insight."[4] We must find a way to fulfill our calling faithfully and with excellence, doing so simultaneously with the Western and Christian traditions.

## A Spiritual Calling

The founders of Harvard College published a pamphlet in 1643 containing their mission statement:

> Let every Student be plainly instructed, and earnestly pressed, to consider well [that] the maine end of his life and studies is to know God and Jesus Christ which is eternall life, Jn 17:3, and therefore to lay Christ in the bottome, as the only foundation of all sound knowledge and Learning.[5]

Other Ivy League schools had similar Christian foundations that enabled them to view their colleges as uni-versities, places of learning in which one could find a uni-ty of truth—a unity that revolved around a God who created all things, who sustains all things such that they consist in him, and who endowed man with the ability to learn about what he created.

We concur that learning is best done from within a Christian framework. Cornelius Plantinga, Dean of Calvin College, writes, "Learning is therefore a *spiritual* calling: properly done, it attaches us to God. In addition, the learned person has, so to speak, more to be Christian *with*."[6] Indeed, we should want to "knead the yeast of the gospel" (as Plantinga puts it) through everything that happens on campus, so that all of a student's rational, creative, and relational capacities would be "permeated with the spirit and teaching of Christianity."[7]

Because of the relevance of Christianity for teaching and learning, the Christian community should: (1) build colleges and research universities; (2) encourage Christian scholars to teach in state universities and other private universities that do not integrate Christian faith and learning, in order to be a faithful Christian presence in those places; and (3) encourage our young people to glorify God in their studies.

## Action Points

- Think back to your educational experience. What encounters did you have with people who were hostile to a Christian worldview or who tolerated it as long as you kept it private? What were some of the reasons they gave against your beliefs? How did they argue for theirs?

- What are the ways that academic studies and scholarship can be worshipful to God? What does that mean for your studies, whether they include formal education, your own private studies, or your charge to teach others in your vocation?

- All of knowledge is unified. This is one of the most significant claims that separate Christians from the rest of the Western academic context today. In what way can we claim that knowledge is unified? What are some things in your life that seem to have little relation to your faith (like washing a cat)? How then do they relate?

## Recommended Reading

Dockery, David. *Renewing Minds: Serving Church and Society through Christian Higher Education.* Nashville: B&H, 2008. An excellent and accessible treatise on how to recover a robust and authentic view of faith and learning.

Holmes, Arthur. *The Idea of a Christian College.* Rev. ed. Grand Rapids: Eerdmans, 1975. An evangelical classic. This slim little volume packs a powerful punch as it sets forth the distinctive mission and contributions of a Christian college.

Marsden, George. *The Outrageous Idea of Christian Scholarship.* Oxford: Oxford University Press, 1997. A 20th-century classic that provides a compelling argument for mainstream American higher education to be open to explicit expressions of faith in an intellectual context.

Noll, Mark. *The Scandal of the Evangelical Mind.* Grand Rapids: Eerdmans, 1994. A compelling argument that evangelicals should value the life of the mind.

Plantinga, Cornelius. *Engaging God's World: A Christian Vision of Faith, Learning, and Living*. Grand Rapids: Eerdmans, 2002. A very accessible interaction with the biblical narrative and its implications for faith, learning, and living.

Wolterstorff, Nicholas. *Educating for Life: Reflections on Christian Teaching and Learning*. Grand Rapids: Baker, 2002. A collection of essays in which Wolterstorff applies his high-octane brain to the notion of faith and learning in Christian high-school education.

———. *Educating for Shalom: Essays on Christian Higher Education*. Grand Rapids: Eerdmans, 2004. A collection of essays in which Wolterstorff reflects upon faith and learning in higher education.

# The Christian Mission

Culture matters to God, and it should matter to us. God created us as profoundly social and cultural beings, and this is what separates us from the animals. When God created Adam and Eve, he told them to be fruitful and multiply, till the soil, and have dominion over all the earth. The command to be fruitful and multiply is a profoundly *social* command, which implied that God wanted humans to build families and communities and societies populated by people who worship him. The commands to till the soil, name the animals, and have dominion are profoundly *cultural* commands. The command to till the soil implied that God wanted people to take his good creation and change it, to make something of it by bringing out its hidden potentials. The command to have dominion states directly that God wanted people to serve as loving managers of his good world (more literally, to serve as vice-regents under God the King), which implies cultural activity. Humanity's mission, therefore, was to spread God's glory across the face of the earth by building societies of worshipers who, in turn, produced cultures that honored God.

The story of humanity took a dark turn when Adam and Eve sinned against God. Satan had tempted Adam and Eve by speaking a word against God's word. He tempted them to question God's word and God's goodness. He tempted them to take upon themselves the qualities of God in order to make their own decisions about right and wrong. They succumbed to the temptation, and the consequences of that sin remain today. After Adam and Eve's sin, all human beings have sinned against God. There is not one corner of society or culture that is left untainted by sin and its consequences. All human beings are alienated from God and from each other, and our social and cultural activities are corrupted and misdirected by sin.

In response to our sin, God sent his Son to atone for our sins. He shed his blood on the cross on our behalf, taking upon himself God's wrath against sin, so that we would not have to pay the consequences of our own sin and so that we could be reconciled to God. Additionally, Christ will redeem and restore the heavens and earth, so that in a future era we will be able to live together with him in an environment whose society and culture is not corrupted by sin.

In light of the fall and God's offer to humanity of a great salvation, our mission now takes on added dimensions. Before the fall, our mission was to spread God's glory across the face of the earth by building societies of worshipers who lived their cultural lives to his glory. After the fall, we retain the original mission, but also have to deal with the ugly fact of sin. This changes the mission in two ways. First, we now have the privilege and responsibility of speaking the good news about Christ's salvation so that our neighbors can believe and be saved from their sin. Second, it means that we have to identify the ways in which our societies and cultures have been corrupted and misdirected by sin, so that we can work to redirect them toward Christ.

## Word and Deed

As we seek to live "redirective" lives, we will find that we must do so with a powerful combination of words and deeds. The Christian life was never meant to be merely words or merely deeds. Whenever we lean too heavily on one and minimize the other, we distort and derail the mission.

One of the strengths of many evangelical Christians is their belief in the centrality of God's Word and of human words to communicate the gospel. Words are absolutely vital to the Christian mission; without them we cannot communicate Christ and the gospel. However, sometimes evangelicals speak about the "priority" of word over deed in such a manner that it seems like they're saying, "Well, if I had to choose between words and actions, I'd choose words." But this is unhelpful. It's like saying, "Well, if I have to choose between telling my neighbor about Jesus and refraining from serial adultery, I'd choose to tell the neighbor about Jesus." But we don't have a choice between verbal evangelism and faithfulness to our spouse. Similarly, the Christian community should not choose between speaking the gospel, on the one hand, and participating in social ministries and cultural activities, on the other.

Another one of the strengths of other evangelical Christians is their belief that the Christian faith ought to be lived out. These Christians recognize the hypocrisy of speaking the gospel without obeying Christ. They participate in social ministries and seek to redirect culture toward Christ. However, sometimes they focus so much on the social and cultural aspects of our obedience that they seem to be choosing actions over words.

It's as if they're saying, "Well, the people around me have had Christianity crammed down their throats for so long that I'm going to focus my energies on *showing* people the way that Christ brings change to a person's life socially and culturally." But this is profoundly unhelpful. Unless your neighbor has the gospel spoken to her, she will not know how to interpret your actions.

## True and False Worship

What is at stake here? Nothing less than true and false worship. Nothing in a culture is entirely neutral. Cultural institutions are either directed toward Christ or against him, or perhaps they are an inconsistent mixture of the two. When God's people neglect cultural engagement, they do so to the detriment of society. To ignore culture is to ignore the cultural institutions that shape people's lives and that will point people either toward Christ or against him.

James K. A. Smith recognizes this reality when he speaks about "secular liturgies." We are familiar with the word "liturgy." When we speak of liturgy, we are speaking of a set of rituals and words used in public worship, usually in a Christian church's worship service. However, any set of practices becomes a liturgy when it plays a significant role in shaping our identity. Secular institutions are liturgical because they provide a matrix of practices and rituals that inculcate a certain (un-Christian) vision of the good life. They misdirect our loves and desires. They skew our basic attunement to this world by pointing us away from Christ and toward a certain idol or cluster of idols.

Smith argues that the mall is a fine example of a cultural institution with a secular liturgy. The mall is a concentrated and intense location for the practices and rituals associated with consumerism. For many people, the mall functions as their primary place of worship. It holds out a certain vision of the good life: "the hip, happy people that populate television commercials are the moving icons of the consumer gospel, illustrations of what the good life looks like: carefree and independent, clean and sexy, perky and perfect."[1] This vision is communicated by the mall's "evangelists"—TV commercials, magazine displays, and Internet advertising.

People who worship at the mall are those who are drawn to its vision of the good life. They compare themselves to the carefree, sexy, perfect people portrayed in the ads and decide that they must shop in order to become more like those people. Implicit in their shopping, therefore, is the idea that the mall provides a certain sort of redemption—a salvation acquired by purchasing goods and enjoying services. The mall's liturgy, therefore, is antithetical to Christian liturgy because the mall's vision of the good life is different from the Christian vision of human flourishing, and its salvation is an alternative to the salvation provided in Christ.

As Christians, therefore, we want to take advantage of every opportunity to shape our cultural activities toward Christ. If the Christian community neglects the cultural aspect of its mission, in effect it is saying, "To hell with culture!" But we cannot do this. Every cultural activity is an opportunity to practice discipleship, to employ words and deeds in Christ's service, to orient our lives toward Christ.

## Three Questions

It can be overwhelming to think about obeying Christ culturally because of how tall a task it is. Practically everything we encounter in the world is cultural. Culture encompasses the totality of our lives, including our eating and drinking, our work and our leisure, and our life inside the church and our life out in the community. It includes not only the aspects of culture we've addressed in this book—art, science, politics, economics, and education—but also ones that we've not addressed, such as homemaking, business and entrepreneurship, and sports and competition. How can we ever get a handle on this tall task?

To live out the cultural aspect of our mission, we should ask three questions every time we find ourselves engaging a certain realm of culture:

- What is God's creational design for this realm of culture?

- How has it been corrupted and misdirected by our sin and rebellion?

- How can I bring healing and redirection to this realm?[2]

Although we might find it easy to remember these questions, and even though they do help us get a handle on the task, we will find that the answers to these questions usually do not come easily.

We must ask God to empower us and give us wisdom, and we must work hard to figure out how to apply God's redemptive word to the cultural realities around us.

## Action Points

- Throughout this book, we've attempted to relate the notion of culture to the Christian mission, arguing that our cultural activities should be oriented toward Christ as a matter of witness and obedience. In your own words, summarize these things and share your response with someone else. As you prepare for that, what concepts seem most clear to you? What things seem cloudy? In light of all that we have discussed, where can you go for answers?

- Make a list of the areas of culture in which you're currently engaged. Of those areas, are there some in which you feel the Lord is calling you to reconsider your obedience and witness? As you join God's mission, what new areas of culture do you feel he is inviting you to launch out into?

## Recommended Reading

Ashford, Bruce Riley, ed. *Theology and Practice of Mission: God, the Church, and the Nations*. Nashville: B&H, 2011. A compendium of essays arguing that a Christian view of mission should take into account the whole biblical storyline, should combine words and deeds, and should emphasize the need to take the gospel to the ends of the earth.

Dickson, John. *The Best Kept Secret of Christian Mission*. Grand Rapids: Zondervan, 2010. A well-written introductory treatment of Christian mission, emphasizing the need to promote the gospel with words and deeds.

Wolters, Albert M. *Creation Regained: Biblical Basics for a Reformational Worldview*. 2nd ed. Grand Rapids: Eerdmans, 2005. A narrative treatment of the biblical worldview, making the connection between the biblical storyline, the Christian worldview, and the Christian mission.

Wright, Christopher J. H. *The Mission of God's People: A Biblical Theology of the Church's Mission*. Grand Rapids: Zondervan, 2010. This is a brief and accessible book on the Christian mission written by a world-class mission theologian. Emphasizes that our mission includes verbal, social, and cultural aspects.

# Recommended Reading Summary

Ashford, Bruce Riley, ed. *Theology and Practice of Mission: God, the Church, and the Nations.* Nashville: B&H, 2011. A compendium of essays arguing that a Christian view of mission should take into account the whole biblical storyline, should combine words and deeds, and should emphasize the need to take the gospel to the ends of the earth.

Audi, Robert and Nicholas Wolterstorff. *Religion in the Public Square: The Place of Religious Convictions in Public Debate.* Lanham, MD: Rowman & Littlefield, 1997. A somewhat technical discussion of Christian convictions and the ways in which believers should dialogue in the public square. Audi argues that Christians should appear "naked" in the public square, while Wolterstorff (himself a political liberal), argues that they should come "fully clothed."

Behe, Michael J. *Darwin's Black Box: The Biochemical Challenge to Evolution.* New York: Touchstone, 1996. A fetching read by a working biochemist about a central problem with Darwinian theory. The book is technical but accessible to the lay reader.

Brand, Chad. *Flourishing Faith: A Baptist Primer on Work, Economics, and Civic Stewardship*. Grand Rapids: Christian's Library Press, 2012. This book is the most concise and accessible primer I know of that addresses work, economics, and civic stewardship.

Budziszewski, J. *Evangelicals in the Public Square: Four Formative Voices on Political Thought and Action*. Grand Rapids: Baker Academic, 2006. This intermediate-to-advanced book describes the way four theologians—Carl Henry, Abraham Kuyper, Francis Schaeffer, and John Howard Yoder—approached the public square.

Carlson, Richard F., ed. *Science and Christianity: Four Views*. Downers Grove, IL: InterVarsity Press, 2000. This book offers four views on the relationship of science and Christianity: Creationism, Independence, Qualified Agreement, and Partnership.

Chang, Curtis. *Engaging Unbelief: A Captivating Strategy from Augustine and Aquinas*. Downers Grove, IL: InterVarsity Press, 2000. A brief reflection on the way Augustine and Thomas Aquinas engaged unbelief in their respective cultural contexts.

Corbett, Steve and Brian Fikkert. *When Helping Hurts: How to Alleviate Poverty Without Hurting the Poor... and Yourself*. Chicago: Moody, 2009. The authors lay a foundation for social ministry and poverty alleviation by defining Jesus' gospel and mission. From there, they show how social ministry and poverty alleviation can be accomplished without hurting the poor or hurting the church.

Crouch, Andy. *Culture Making: Recovering our Creative Calling*. Downers Grove, IL: InterVarsity Press, 2008. An engaging and persuasive treatise on the Christian community's calling to "make culture" rather than merely "engage the culture."

Davis, John Jefferson. *The Frontiers of Science and Faith*. Downers Grove, IL: InterVarsity Press, 2002. A terrific exploration of 10 current scientific issues and their intersection with Christian theology and life.

Dickson, John. *The Best Kept Secret of Christian Mission*. Grand Rapids: Zondervan, 2010. A well-written introductory treatment of Christian mission, emphasizing the need to promote the gospel with words and deeds.

Dockery, David. *Renewing Minds: Serving Church and Society through Christian Higher Education*. Nashville: B&H, 2008. An excellent and accessible treatise on how to recover a robust and authentic view of faith and learning.

Duriez, Colin. *Francis Schaeffer: An Authentic Life*. Wheaton, IL: Crossway, 2008. A biography of Francis Schaeffer, written by a man who knew Schaeffer well.

Forster, Greg. *Joy for the World: How Christianity Lost Its Cultural Influence and Can Begin Rebuilding It*. Wheaton, IL: Crossway, 2014. A well-written and easy-to-read book arguing that the key to cultural transformation is Spirit-induced joy in God and the gospel.

Gallagher, Susan V. and Roger Lundin. *Literature Through the Eyes of Faith*. New York: HarperCollins: 1989. An excellent introduction that shows how reading literature helps us interpret our lives.

Godawa, Brian. *Hollywood Worldviews: Watching Films with Wisdom and Discernment*. 2nd ed. Downers Grove, IL: InterVarsity

Press, 2009. An engaging book that equips readers to watch films critically.

Goheen, Mike and Craig Bartholomew. *Living at the Crossroads: An Introduction to Christian Worldview.* Grand Rapids: Baker Academic, 2008. This book is a fine treatment of how the biblical narrative fosters a worldview that in turn shapes the entirety of the Christian life, including especially culture-making and cultural engagement.

Grudem, Wayne. *Business for the Glory of God.* Wheaton, IL: Crossway, 2003. A short introduction to the Bible's teaching on the moral goodness of business and entrepreneurship.

Holmes, Arthur. *The Idea of a Christian College.* Rev. ed. Grand Rapids: Eerdmans, 1975. An evangelical classic. This slim little volume packs a powerful punch as it sets forth the distinctive mission and contributions of a Christian college.

Hunter, James Davison. *To Change the World: Irony, Tragedy, and Possibility of Christianity in the Late Modern World.* Oxford: Oxford University Press, 2010. A sociologist argues that Christians should aim to be a "faithful presence" in their culture.

Keathley, Kenneth D., and Mark F. Rooker, *40 Questions about Creation and Evolution.* Grand Rapids: Kregel, 2014. This is the best one-stop introduction to the contested question of the relationship between creation and evolution.

Keller, Timothy. *Every Good Endeavor: Connecting Your Work to God's Work.* New York: Penguin, 2012. A more extensive treatment of the Christian view of work.

Kuyper, Abraham. *Lectures on Calvinism.* 1898. Reprint, Grand Rapids: Eerdmans, 1943. In this small book, Kuyper argues that our Christianity should affect every sphere of human life and culture.

Lester DeKoster and Stephen Grabill. *Work: The Meaning of Your Life.* 2nd ed. Grand Rapids: Christian's Library Press, 2010. A very short book introducing the Christian understanding of work.

Markos, Louis. *Lewis Agonistes: How C. S. Lewis Can Train Us to Wrestle with the Modern and Postmodern World.* Nashville: B&H, 2003. An exposition of what Lewis can teach us about engaging with art, science, philosophy, and other realms of culture.

Marsden, George. *The Outrageous Idea of Christian Scholarship.* Oxford: Oxford University Press, 1997. A 20th-century classic that provides a compelling argument for mainstream American higher education to be open to explicit expressions of faith in an intellectual context.

Moore, T. M. *Culture Matters: A Call for Consensus on Christian Cultural Engagement.* Grand Rapids: Brazos, 2007. A helpful introduction to the ways in which some Christians have engaged their respective cultures.

Mouw, Richard J. *Abraham Kuyper: A Short and Personal Introduction.* Grand Rapids: Eerdmans, 2011. An excellent little introduction to Kuyper's life and thought.

———. *Called to Holy Worldliness.* Philadelphia: Fortress, 1980. A small book showing how ordinary Christians can honor God in their culture-making and cultural engagement.

———. *Uncommon Decency: Christian Civility in an Uncivil World.* 2nd ed. Downers Grove, IL: InterVarsity Press, 2010. An argument that Christians should bring not only their Christian convictions to the public square, but also their Christian virtue—especially the ability to be civil in the midst of debate and discussion.

Mouw, Richard J. and Sander Griffioen. *Pluralisms and Horizons: An Essay in Christian Public Philosophy*. Grand Rapids: Eerdmans, 1993. An unpacking of the problem of political consensus in a pluralist environment, which includes a helpful comparison and contrast of major thinkers on the topic, including John Rawls, Robert Nozick, and Richard John Neuhaus.

Neuhaus, Richard John. *The Naked Public Square: Religion and Democracy in America*. Grand Rapids: Eerdmans, 1984. A very influential and well-argued text on the place of Christian conviction in public political discourse.

Niebuhr, H. Richard. *Christ and Culture*. New York: HarperCollins, 1956. This text has become the modern benchmark for discussing Christianity and culture. It has flaws—serious ones—but is worth reading.

Noll, Mark. *The Scandal of the Evangelical Mind*. Grand Rapids: Eerdmans, 1994. A compelling argument that evangelicals should value the life of the mind.

Novak, Michael. *The Spirit of Democratic Capitalism*. Lanham, MD: Madison, 1991. A vigorous examination of capitalism and democracy with a particularly good articulation of a "theology of democratic capitalism."

O'Connor, Flannery. "The Church and the Fiction Writer" in *Mystery and Manners*, 143–53. New York: Farrar, Straus, and Giroux, 1961. An essay providing insight into the relationship of faith and writing.

Pearcy, Nancy R. and Charles B. Thaxton. *The Soul of Science: Christian Faith and Natural Philosophy*. Wheaton, IL: Crossway, 1994. An analysis of the way in which Judaeo-Christian thought funds the scientific enterprise, including a look at mathematics and scientific "revolutions," and the discipline called the "History of Science."

Plantinga, Alvin. *Where the Conflict Really Lies: Science, Religion, and Naturalism.* Oxford: Oxford University Press, 2011. An argument that there is deep resonance between Christianity and science, and deep conflict between atheism and science. Advanced.

Plantinga, Cornelius. *Engaging God's World: A Christian Vision of Faith, Learning, and Living.* Grand Rapids: Eerdmans, 2002. A very accessible interaction with the biblical narrative and its implications for faith, learning, and living.

Poythress, Vern. *Redeeming Science: A God-Centered Approach.* Wheaton, IL: Crossway, 2006. An argument that Christianity, theology, and science are mutually beneficial dialogue partners.

Richards, Jay W. *Infiltrated: How to Stop the Insiders and Activists Who Are Exploiting the Financial Crisis to Control Our Lives and Our Fortunes.* New York: McGraw Hill, 2013. A deft exposé of big-government economic regulation and the crippling effects of cronyism.

———. *Money, Greed, and God: Why Capitalism Is the Solution and Not the Problem.* New York: HarperCollins, 2009. An excellent argument that Christians can and should work from within the free-market economy (rather than viewing it as evil) to help our world flourish.

Rookmaaker, H. R. *Modern Art and the Death of a Culture.* 2nd ed. Leicester: Inter-Varsity Press, 1973. A modern classic that offers penetrating insight into modern art and the intellectual context beneath it. Advanced.

Schaeffer, Francis A. *Art and the Bible: Two Essays*. Rev. ed. Downers Grove, IL: InterVarsity Press, 2006. A small book encapsulating Schaeffer's approach to the arts.

Seerveld, Calvin. *Bearing Fresh Olive Leaves: Alternative Steps in Understanding Art*. Toronto: Piquant, 2000. An advanced treatment of how Christians can understand, make, perform, and evaluate the arts.

Smith, James K. A. *Desiring the Kingdom*. Grand Rapids: Baker Academic, 2009. An advanced book which argues that secular "liturgies" compete with Christian liturgies in order to shape who we are and form our deepest identities and views of the world.

Veith, Gene Edward Jr. *State of the Arts: From Bezalel to Mapplethorpe*. Wheaton, IL: Crossway, 1991. A useful introduction to understanding the biblical foundations for art and the broad contours of contemporary art.

———. *God at Work: Your Christian Vocation in All of Life*. Wheaton, IL: Crossway, 2011. A short book introducing the Christian's calling to church, family, workplace, and community.

Wittmer, Michael E. *Heaven Is a Place on Earth: Why Everything You Do Matters to God*. Grand Rapids: Zondervan, 2004. A very accessible treatment of the Bible's teaching about culture.

Wolters, Albert M. *Creation Regained: Biblical Basics for a Reformational Worldview*. 2nd ed. Grand Rapids: Eerdmans, 2005. A narrative treatment of the biblical worldview, making the connection between the biblical storyline, the Christian worldview, and the Christian mission.

Wolterstorff, Nicholas. *Art in Action: Toward a Christian Aesthetic*. Grand Rapids: Eerdmans, 1980. A Christian philosophy of art arguing that art has a legitimate and necessary place in everyday life. Advanced.

———. *Educating for Life: Reflections on Christian Teaching and Learning*. Grand Rapids: Baker, 2002. A collection of essays in which Wolterstorff applies his high-octane brain to the notion of faith and learning in Christian high-school education.

———. *Educating for Shalom: Essays on Christian Higher Education*. Grand Rapids: Eerdmans, 2004. A collection of essays in which Wolterstorff reflects on faith and learning in higher education.

Wright, Christopher J. H. *The Mission of God's People: A Biblical Theology of the Church's Mission*. Grand Rapids: Zondervan, 2010. This is a brief and accessible book on the Christian mission written by a world-class mission theologian. Emphasizes that our mission includes verbal, social, and cultural aspects.

## Introduction

1. Kuyper spoke these words during his inaugural address at the Free University of Amsterdam, which he founded. His remarks can be found in Kuyper, "Sphere Sovereignty," in *Abraham Kuyper: A Centennial Reader*, ed. James D. Bratt (Grand Rapids: Eerdmans, 1998), 488.
2. From an excerpt translated by Jan Boer, *You Can Do Greater Things than Christ* (Nigeria: Jos, 1991).
3. http://www.firstthings.com/article/2007/04/christ-without-culture

## Chapter 2: A Theology of Culture

1. John Calvin, *The Institutes*, I.15.3.
2. In this context, dualism refers to the belief that life can be divided into two isolated spheres (the physical world and the spiritual world), with one sphere usually viewed as superior to the other. Unfortunately, many Christians have divided the world into material and immaterial aspects, and viewed the immaterial (spiritual) world as superior to the material world.
3. Al Wolters, *Creation Regained*, 2nd ed. (Grand Rapids: Eerdmans, 2005), 87–114.
4. Dietrich Bonhoeffer, *Letters and Papers From Prison*, Enlarged ed. (New York: Macmillan, 1972), 336–7.

## Chapter 3: Culture and Calling

1. For a very readable and interesting book on these vocations, I recommend Gene Veith's *God at Work: Your Christian Vocation in All of Life* (Wheaton, IL: Crossway, 2002).
2. Veith, *God at Work*, 78.
3. John Stott, "Reclaiming the Biblical Doctrine of Work," *Christianity Today*, May 4, 1979, 37.

## Chapter 4: Six Case Studies on Culture

1. The best abridged edition for contemporary readers is Augustine, *City of God*, ed. Vernon J. Bourke, trans. Gerald Walsh, Demetrius Zema, Grace Monahan, and Daniel Honan (New York: Image, 1958).

2. Curtis Chang, *Engaging Unbelief: A Captivating Strategy from Augustine and Aquinas* (Downers Grove, IL: InterVarsity Press, 2000), 66–93.

3. For a sample of Kuyper's writings, see Abraham Kuyper, *Lectures on Calvinism* (Grand Rapids: Eerdmans, 1931). A very brief but excellent exposition of his life and writings is Richard Mouw, *Abraham Kuyper: A Short and Personal introduction* (Grand Rapids: Eerdmans, 2011). A more extended exposition is James D. Bratt, *Abraham Kuyper: Modern Calvinist, Christian Democrat* (Grand Rapids: Eerdmans, 2013).

4. C. S. Lewis, "Is Theology Poetry?" in *The Weight of Glory* (San Francisco: HarperCollins, 2001), 140.

5. Michael Travers, "We Are Made for Heaven: An Introduction to C. S. Lewis" (paper presented at the L. Russ Bush Center for Faith & Culture, Wake Forest, NC, October 22, 2010).

6. I owe this Dorothy Sayers section to Andrew Spencer, who did the majority of the research and writing for it.

7. Nancy Marie Patterson Tischler, *Dorothy L. Sayers, a Pilgrim Soul* (Atlanta: John Knox, 1980), 141.

8. Tischler, *Dorothy L. Sayers*, 102.

9. Letter from Dr. Welch dated Dec 30, 1940, cited in James Brabazon, *Dorothy L. Sayers* (New York: HarperCollins, 1982), 199.

10. Letter to Dr. Welch dated Jan 2, 1941, cited in Brabazon, *Dorothy L. Sayers*, 199.

11. Dorothy L. Sayers, *Gaudy Night* (New York: Harper Paperbacks, 1995), 332–33.

12. Dorothy L. Sayers, *The Mind of the Maker* (London: Methuen, 1952), vii.

13. Sayers, *Mind of the Maker*, ix.

14. Sayers *Mind of the Maker*, 7.

15. The speech Sayers delivered to the Archbishop of York's conference in Malvern, 1941, is one of the sources that make clear that Sayers held something like a transformationalist view. Dorothy L. Sayers, "The Church's Responsibility," in *Malvern, 1941: The Life of the Church and the Order of Society : Being the Proceedings of the Archbishop of York's Conference* (London: Longmans Green, 1941), 57–78.

16. See also Brabazon, *Dorothy L. Sayers,* 189.

17. Colin Duriez, *Francis Schaeffer: An Authentic Life* (Wheaton, IL: Crossway, 2008), 136. Duriez interviewed Priscilla in 2007.

18. Duriez, *Francis Schaeffer,* 145.

19. Duriez, *Francis Schaeffer*, 9.

## Chapter 5: The Arts

1. Francis A. Schaeffer, *Art and the Bible* (Downers Grove, IL: InterVarsity Press, 2006).

2. Nicholas Wolterstorff, *Art in Action* (Carlisle, UK: Solway, 1997), 4.

3. Although our creativity will in some ways be similar to God's, it also remains fundamentally different. While God created his own material which he then shaped artfully, we must borrow God's material in order to be artful and creative.

4. Hans Urs von Balthasar, *The Glory of the Lord* (Edinburgh: T&T Clark, 1983), 1:131.

5. Hans R. Rookmaaker, *Art Needs No Justification* (Vancouver: Regent College, 1978), 40.

6. Dorothy Sayers, "Toward a Christian Aesthetic," in *Christian Letters to a Post-Christian World*, ed. Roderick Jellema (Grand Rapids: Eerdmans, 1969), 69.

7. Colin Gunton, foreword to *Voicing Creation's Praise: Towards a Theology of the Arts*, by Jeremy S. Begbie (Edinburgh: T&T Clark, 1991), xii.

8. Abraham Kuyper, *Lectures on Calvinism* (Grand Rapids: Eerdmans, 1943), 229.

9. Jeremy S. Begbie, *Beholding the Glory: Incarnation through the Arts* (Grand Rapids: Baker Academic, 2001), xiii.

## Chapter 6: The Sciences

1. Nancy R. Pearcey and Charles B. Thaxton, *The Soul of Science: Christian Faith and Natural Philosophy* (Wheaton, IL: Crossway, 1994), 18–20.

2. Pearcey and Thaxton, *The Soul of Science*, 21.

3. Richard Dawkins is a prominent scientist who argues that science and theology are incompatible. See Richard Dawkins, *The God Delusion* (New York: Houghton Mifflin, 2006).

4. Stephen Barr, "Retelling the Story of Science," *First Things* 131 (March 2003): 16–25.

5. Barr would have been better served to say that naturalism (rather than materialism) is in conflict with theology. Although naturalism and materialism are nearly the same, materialists can be theists in some sense (e.g., Thomas Hobbes) or can be open to supernatural emphases, even if they define "supernatural" differently. Naturalism, however, asserts that all things are physical and that God does not exist. In short, naturalism entails materialism but goes beyond it to atheism.

6. David Clark, *To Know and Love God* (Wheaton, IL: Crossway, 2003), 284.

7. This list is a slight modification of the five points presented by Clark, *To Know and Love God*, 287–94.

8. John Polkinghorne, *Scientists as Theologians* (London: SPCK, 1996), 6–7.

9. For a fascinating treatment of this historical debate, see Kenneth D. Keathley, "Flat or Round? The Sixth Century Debate," in *Intelligent Design: William A. Dembski and Michael Ruse in Dialogue*, ed. Robert Stewart (Minneapolis: Augsburg Fortress, 2007), 196–209.

## Chapter 7: Politics and the Public Square

1. John Rawls, *A Theory of Justice*, rev. ed. (Cambridge, MA: Belknap, 1999).

2. Os Guinness, *The Global Public Square: Religious Freedom and the Making of a World Safe for Diversity* (Downers Grove, IL: InterVarsity Press, 2013), 69.

3. Abraham Kuyper, *Lectures on Calvinism*, 97 (see ch. 4, n. 3). Richard J. Mouw, "Some Reflections on Sphere Sovereignty," in *Religion, Pluralism, and Public Life: Abraham Kuyper's Legacy for the Twenty-First Century*, ed. Luis E. Lugo (Grand Rapids: Eerdmans, 2000), 87–109.

4. Richard Mouw, *Political Evangelism* (Grand Rapids: Eerdmans, 1973), 55.

5. Mouw, *He Shines in All That's Fair: Culture and Common Grace* (Grand Rapids: Eerdmans, 2001), 76–87.

6. Mouw, *Political Evangelism*, 76–85.

7. Mouw, *Uncommon Decency: Christian Civility in an Uncivil World*, rev. and exp. ed. (Grand Rapids: InterVarsity Press, 2010), 33–38.

## Chapter 8: Economics and Wealth

1. Karl Marx and Friedrich Engels, "The Communist Manifesto," in Karl Marx, *Selected Writings*, ed. Lawrence H. Simon (Indianapolis: Hackett, 1994), 158–59.
2. Marx and Engels, "Communist Manifesto," 158–86.
3. For a brief summary of von Mises' points, articulated from a Christian point of view, see Ronald Nash, *Social Justice and the Christian Church* (Lima, OH: Academic Renewal Press, 2002), 91–102.
4. Michael Novak, *The Spirit of Democratic Capitalism* (Lanham, MD: Madison, 1991).
5. For further reading, see Jay Wesley Richards, *Infiltrated: How to Stop the Insiders and Activists Who Are Exploiting the Financial Crisis to Control Our Lives and Our Fortunes* (Chicago: McGraw-Hill, 2013).

## Chapter 9: Scholarship and Education

1. David Dockery, *Renewing Minds* (Nashville: B&H, 2008), xiii.
2. George Marsden, *The Outrageous Idea of Christian Scholarship* (Oxford: Oxford University Press, 1997), 7. Marsden cites John Green's quote in Peter Steinfels, "Universities Biased against Religion, Scholar Says," *The New York Times*, November 26, 1993, A22.
3. Marsden, *Outrageous Idea*, 7.
4. Michael W. Goheen and Craig G. Bartholomew, *Living at the Crossroads: An Introduction to Christian Worldview* (Grand Rapids: Baker Academic, 2008), 163.
5. "New England's First Fruits," quoted in Perry Miller and Thomas H. Johnson, *The Puritans* (New York: American Book, 1938), 702.
6. Cornelius Plantinga, *Engaging God's World: A Christian View of Faith, Learning, and Living* (Grand Rapids: Eerdmans, 2002), xi, xiii.
7. Plantinga, *Engaging God's World*, xiii.

## Conclusion: The Christian Mission

1. James K. A. Smith, *Desiring the Kingdom* (Grand Rapids: Baker Academic, 2009), 95.
2. Michael W. Goheen and Craig G. Bartholomew, *Living at the Crossroads: An Introduction to Christian Worldview* (Grand Rapids: Baker, 2008), 138–39.

# SCRIPTURE INDEX

## Old Testament

## New Testament